THE POETRY OF RAFAEL ALBERTI
A VISUAL APPROACH

ROBERT C. MANTEIGA

THE POETRY
OF RAFAEL ALBERTI:
A VISUAL APPROACH

TAMESIS BOOKS LIMITED
LONDON

Colección Támesis
SERIE A - MONOGRAFIAS, LXXV

Depósito Legal: M. 7861 - 1979
Printed in Spain by Talleres Gráficos de SELECCIONES GRÁFICAS (EDICIONES)
Paseo de la Dirección, 52 - Madrid-29

for
TAMESIS BOOKS LIMITED
LONDON

Table of Contents

Acknowledgements

I would like to express my sincerest gratitude to Professor B. Bussell Thompson for making available to me the Casa Hispánica's collection of materials on Rafael Alberti, to Dr. Arnold A. del Greco for his patience and unselfish dedication, and to Don Germán Bleiberg for his helpful advice and encouragement.

A ti, sonoro, puro, quieto, blando
incalculable al mar de la paleta,
por quien la neta luz, la sombra neta
en su trasmutación pasan soñando.

A ti, por quien la vida combinando
color y color busca ser concreta;
metamorfosis de la forma, meta
del paisaje tranquilo o caminando.

A ti, armónica lengua, cielo abierto,
descompasado dios, orden, concierto,
raudo relieve, lisa investidura.

Los posibles en ti nunca se acaban.
Las materias sin términos te alaban.
A ti, gloria y pasión de la Pintura.

RAFAEL ALBERTI

Introduction

Rafael Alberti began his poetic career in 1924 and continues to be, more than a half century later, one of the most prolific writers of his poetic generation. In the words of Ricardo Gullón, to read the works of Alberti from 1924 to 1962 is to study the evolution of contemporary poetry in full.[1] Nevertheless, he has not achieved the recognition he deserves. We can cite at least five recognized works on contemporary Spanish poetry in which there is little mention of Alberti, and in which few if any of his writings appear.[2]

In addition to being often ignored, Alberti's literary critics have not always treated him favorably or in depth. For example, Angel del Río, contrasting briefly Alberti with Lorca, says: «En Alberti todo es claro, como producto de una inteligencia poética de primer orden, pero inteligencia fría, aunque la naturalidad con que se consigue el verso perfecto deje la impresión de una suma espontaneidad.»[3] Torrente Ballester adds that «la dimensión profunda falta en la poesía de Alberti, quien jamás se ha zambullido en su propia oscuridad, pero que, en cambio, supo y pudo siempre aparentar.»[4]

Although Alberti's contributions in the field of poetry have been of major significance, it is appropriate to say that relatively little has been written about him. However, worthy of note are: a number of articles[5]

---

[1] RICARDO GULLÓN, «Alegrías y sombras de Rafael Alberti,» *Insula*, 198 (May 1963), p. 1.

[2] DÁMASO ALONSO, *Poetas españoles contemporáneos* (Madrid: Gredos, 1958).— JOSÉ LUIS CANO, *De Machado a Bousoño* (Madrid: Insula, 1955); *Poesía española del siglo XX* (Madrid: Guadarrama, 1960).—LUIS CERNUDA, *Estudios sobre la poesía española* (Madrid: Guadarrama, 1957).—ANGEL DEL RÍO, *Estudios sobre la literatura contemporánea española* (Madrid: Gredos, 1966).

[3] ANGEL DEL RÍO, *Historia de la literatura española* (New York: Dryden Press, 1948), II, p. 260.

[4] GONZALO TORRENTE BALLESTER, *Literatura española contemporánea* (Madrid: Aguado, 1949), p. 434.

[5] Among especially informative studies are the following: G. W. CONNELL, «The Autobiographical Elements in *Sobre los ángeles*,» *Bulletin of Spanish Studies*, 40 (1963), pp. 160-173; «A Recurring Theme in the Poetry of Rafael Alberti,» *Renaissance and Modern Studies*, 3 (1959), pp. 95-110.—C. B. MORRIS, «Las imágenes claves de *Sobre los ángeles*,» *Insula*, 198 (May 1963), p. 12.—ERIC PROLL, «Popularismo and Barroquismo in the Poetry of Rafael Alberti,» *Bulletin of Spanish Studies*, 14 (1942), pp. 59-86; «The Surrealist Element in Rafael Alberti,» *Bulletin of Spanish Studies*, 18 (1941), pp. 70-82.—SOLITA SALINAS DE MARICHAL, «Los paraísos perdidos de Rafael Alberti,» *Insula*, 198 (May 1963), p. 10.—LORENZO VARELA, «En el aire

treating his poetry, Emilia de Zuleta's *Cinco poetas españoles*,[6] Solita Salinas de Marichal's volume,[7] and José Luis Tejada's study.[8] In the majority of these works, the attention devoted to the elements is minimal and the theme of color and color symbolism is either of parenthetical value or avoided as a main consideration. Salinas de Marichal studies only Alberti's earlier works in this vein. Zardoya in «La técnica metafórica albertiana,» links the color theme to the same earlier works while Ana María Winkelman (in her article «Pintura y poesía en Rafael Alberti») stresses only the work *A la pintura*. None of the studies, however, fully examines the manner in which the elements are treated or attempts to establish any relationship between the poet's use of color and the moods created by particular colors or combinations of colors. Therefore, we shall observe the role the elements play in many of Alberti's compositions and see exactly how the poet implements color within this elemental framework. We then shall attempt to establish some correlation between the color patterns which develop within a given work and the mood reflected therein. Alberti's skillful implementation of color and the techniques of color imagery and color symbolism, make him perhaps the most visually oriented poet of the «Grupo de 1927» with the possible exception of García Lorca.

It is not surprising that Alberti's poetry is so visually oriented. Painting was, at one point in his life, Alberti's favorite pastime. In fact, contrary to Ana María Winkelman's claim that Alberti began both hobbies, painting and poetry, simultaneously, his autobiography and other writings reveal that his interest in painting was cultivated earlier: «En un principio buscó en la pintura el medio de expresar sus inquietudes en colores y formas. Luego es la poesía donde hallarán expresión estas inquietudes por medio de la palabra y la metáfora.»[9] Though not mentioned in any of his poems, it was his aunt Lola who was most instrumental in Alberti's artistic development. The approval she expressed upon seeing Rafael's first water colors was a great inspiration to him.[10] When Alberti's family later moved to Madrid, he made numerous friends within the artistic circles. He spent

sonoro de Rafael Alberti,» *Sol* (April 28, 1936); «La flauta y el pito; el tambor y el salmo; y la poesía (en torno a Rafael Alberti),» *Tall,* 10 (1940), pp. 41-45; «Pasión y gracia de Rafael Alberti,» *Roman,* 6 (1940).—Luis Felipe Vivanco, «Rafael Alberti en su palabra acelerada y vestida de luces,» in *Introducción a la poesía española contemporánea* (Madrid: Guadarrama, 1961), pp. 223-258.—Ana María Winkelman, «Pintura y poesía en Rafael Alberti,» *Papeles de Son Armadans,* 88 (1963), pp. 147-162.—Concha Zardoya, «El mar en la poesía de Rafael Alberti,» in *Poesía española contemporánea* (Madrid: Guadarrama, 1961), pp. 600-633; «Rafael Alberti y sus primeras *Poesías completas,»* *Revista Hispánica Moderna,* 30 (1964), pp. 12-19; «La técnica metafórica albertiana,» in *Poesía española del 98 y del 27* (Madrid: Gredos, 1968), pp. 294-336.

   [6] Emilia de Zulueta, *Cinco poetas españoles* (Madrid: Gredos, 1971), pp. 273-396.
   [7] Solita Salinas de Marichal, *El mundo poético de Rafael Alberti* (Madrid: Gredos, 1968).
   [8] José Luis Tejada, *Rafael Alberti, Entre la tradición y la vanguardia* (Madrid: Gredos, 1977).
   [9] Alberto Monterde, «Inquietudes y medievalismo en la poesía de Rafael Alberti,» *Universidad de México,* 9 (1954), p. 8.
   [10] Rafael Alberti, *La Arboleda perdida* (Buenos Aires: Compañía General Fabril Editora, 1959), p. 71.

endless hours studying the paintings in the Prado Museum and admiring in particular the works of Velázquez. Despite a prolonged illness which required rest and medical attention, Rafael would steal away in the evenings from the family's apartment on Lagasca, and sit for hours in front of the Puerta de Alcalá until he captured the effect of the moonlight on the arch.[11]

Although his success as a painter was limited, Alberti did receive some recognition. From José Luis Salado we learn that a few of Rafael Alberti's paintings were displayed in an exhibition at the Ateneo of Madrid: «En 1922 Alberti celebró en el Ateneo una exposición de dibujos. Nada del «Casón» ya. El futuro poeta de *Marinero en tierra* practicaba entonces un tipo de cubismo ingenuo, intuitivo; casi era en esa época, con Rafael Barrados, el único oficiante del cubismo.»[12] The cubist nature of Alberti's painting had great bearing on his poetry. In the opinion of Eric Proll, the geometrical construction of imagery in Alberti's poetry corresponds to the ideals of the cubists in painting,[13] a natural evolution considering Alberti's early artistic inclinations.

For no obvious reason other than his health (Alberti suffered from tuberculosis), he suddenly abandoned painting, and, except for an occasional sketch accompanying one of his poems, did not resume that hobby until late in life. Perhaps the reason for deserting painting is found in Alberto Monterde's statement that: «La poesía ha sido la manifestación que más ha servido para recoger el registro de su personalidad conmocionada.»[14] In reality, Rafael Alberti never completely dismissed this mode of expression. He merely discovered a more flexible means of creating some of the same visual effects. Vicente Aleixandre, in his prologue to Alberti's book *A la pintura,* writes about the crucial period in Alberti's life when he gave up painting to become a poet:

> ¡Qué quince años siguieron! El pincel se secó, se empalideció, fue deshecho. Entre los dedos fríos de Rafael seguía algo como una varita, pero el color del trazo era uniforme: ¡el color de la tinta! Tinta pura y tinta impura. Tinta del mar y tinta de la tierra. Tinta verde del campo, tinta roja de la sangre, y tinta cárdena de la ira, y tinta negra de la muerte. Pero color, súbito y sintético, en blanco, de toda la luz fluyendo, suprema, por el cabo de esa fontana que se sucedía.[15]

Aleixandre was not the only one to notice this quality in Alberti. Dámaso Alonso states in his article, «Rafael entre su Arboleda,» that he had no idea how great an effect Rafael Alberti's brief vocation as a painter had on his poetry: «Sólo hoy, al leer *La Arboleda perdida,* es cuando he com-

---

[11] Ibíd., p. 117.
[12] José Luis Salado, «Rafael Alberti, de niño quería ser pintor,» *Cervantes* (March-April 1931). No page indicated.
[13] Eric Proll, «The Surrealist Element in Rafael Alberti,» *Bulletin of Spanish Studies,* 18 (1941), p. 71.
[14] Alberto Monterde, p. 8.
[15] Vicente Aleixandre, «Rafael Alberti, pintor,» in Rafael Alberti, *Poesía* (1924-1967) (Madrid: Aguilar, 1967), pp. 685-686.

prendido cuánto fue en su vida esta vocación de pintor.»[16] Juan Gaya
Nuño also admires and praises the visual quality of Alberti's work: «Tú,
Rafael Alberti, has convertido la historia y la crítica del arte en género
áureo, en voz sublime que va ondulando de lo más grandioso a lo más
delicado, sintiendo la pintura y viviendo la pintura.»[17] Finally, Miguel
Angel Asturias, Nobel Prize winner in literature, says that Alberti, «sin
dejar de ser un gran poeta, nos baja de las alturas celestes, que sorprende
desde su observatorio sensible, formas y colores que son versos, versos
no escritos, sino dibujados.»[18]

The visual character of Alberti's poetry is achieved through the use
of images which appeal directly to the sense of sight: «... imagen que se di-
rige al ojo ... y que comunica una experiencia semejante a la que se logra
en el arte plástico.»[19] Emilia de Zulueta calls Alberti's images, «imágenes
pictóricas de extremada belleza.»[20] Critics agree that Alberti's preference
for visual images stems from his early interest in painting: «La influencia
de este arte en su formación artística se manifiesta en ciertas imágenes que
aparecen en su poesía y que revelan el ojo del pintor.»[21] «Sus imágenes son
siempre de una plasticidad que las hace merecedoras de tal nombre, y sólo
quien alguna vez haya atisbado la realidad con ojos de pintor está capaci-
tado para captarlas.»[22]

Because of the visual nature of his images, Alberti is considered
somewhat of a rebel in the context of twentieth century poetry.[23] Not all
of his images, however, are strikingly visual. Like other members of his
poetic generation, he dabbled in the new art forms of the Vanguard
movements, and experimented with the metaphor. But, because of his
skillful application of colors, the otherwise abstract images he occasionally
employs are less difficult for the reader to comprehend. «Los colores,»
says Eduardo González Lanuza, «desbordan de sus estrofas, unos colores
manejados con la intimidad de quien los puede llamar por sus nombres
propios, a ellos y a sus matices.»[24]

While a number of scholars have suggested that Alberti employed
colors for purely descriptive purposes, there is evidence to show that this
is not entirely true. «Una lectura más atenta,» states Concha Zardoya,
«nos revela una verdadera cromatología albertiana en la cual se despliegan
colores puros y esenciales, declinan algunos matices simbólicos, o se com-
binan en una pluralización cromática de cadencias ascendentes o descen-

---

[16] Dámaso Alonso, «Rafael entre su Arboleda,» *Insula* 198 (May 1963), p. 1.
[17] Juan Antonio Gaya Nuño, «Carta a Rafael Alberti sobre la pintura,» *Insula* 198
(May 1963), p. 3.
[18] Miguel Angel Asturias, «Rafael Alberti, poeta y pintor,» *El Nacional* (March
19, 1959). No page number.
[19] Winkelman, p. 148.
[20] Emilia de Zuleta, p. 292.
[21] Winkelman, p. 147.
[22] Eduardo González Lanuza, «Crónicas: Homenaje a Rafael Alberti,» *Sur*, 281
(1963), p. 56.
[23] In twentieth century poetry there is a definite trend away from the visual image
and more emphasis is placed on what Carlos Bousoño calls «la imagen visionaria».
[24] González Lanuza, *Crónicas*, p. 56.

dentes, o chocan en fuerte contraste.»[25] We could also add that, whether it is done consciously or subconsciously, Alberti's colors often represent mental processes or moods which continually change as the poet matures.

For our purposes we will not be considering Alberti's work in its entirety. Some of his works are more pertinent to a study on color than others. Emphasis will be placed on such works as *Marinero en tierra, La amante, El alba del alhelí, Cal y canto, Sobre los ángeles, Pleamar, Retornos de lo vivo lejano* and *Baladas y canciones del Paraná,* which contain the substance of this essay. «Toro en el mar,» Part IV of his book *Entre el clavel y la espada,* is added to this list not because the use of color emerges prominently but because therein are reflected images related to Spain and symbolized in a «verde toro.»

Our study will consist of five chapters. The first, «Mar y tierra,» concerns itself with Alberti's early poetry. His first well known volume, *Marinero en tierra,* for which he won the Premio Nacional de Literatura, is a collection of simple poems which offer a panoramic view of life in the port town of Puerto de Santa María. The poems, which mirror a preference for colors and images of a purely descriptive nature, convey a sense of innocence and beauty. *La amante,* Alberti's second book, is a collection of «canciones» written in the popular vein that evoke a more serious mood. *El alba del alhelí,* written primarily in Rute, a small town near Córdoba in the Sierra Morena, is a series of colorful compositions which are much more dramatic than his previous poetry, «Más para la guitarra que para la culta vihuela de las canciones.»[26] The poems herein strike a serious note effectively revealed by the author's introduction of somber hues.

The second chapter, «Aire y fuego,» deals with two of Alberti's more creative works, *Cal y canto* and *Sobre los ángeles.* In each the poet appears more elusive and more intense than in his previous compositions. His inner conflicts (which begin manifesting themselves in *Cal y canto,*) come to the surface in *Sobre los ángeles.* C. M. Bowra, in his book, *The Creative Experiment,* explains that,

> *Sobre los ángeles* is concerned with a terrible crisis in which Alberti finds that for no explicable reason he has lost his trust in himself and his hold on existence, that things which have hitherto meant much to him have suddenly left him, that he has been robbed not merely of his dreams and visions but of everything which gives savour and significance to life, and he does not know what to think or what to do.[27]

Our third chapter, «La sombra de los toros,» treats Alberti's «Poesía taurina.» Alberti sees the bullfight as a microcosm of war, and the colors he employs often evoke feelings of violence and horror. The works in which this theme is most effectively developed are «Toro en el mar» from *Entre el clavel y la espada,* «Egloga fúnebre» from *Pleamar,* and *Verte*

---

[25] CONCHA ZARDOYA, *La técnica metafórica albertiana,* p. 318.
[26] RAFAEL ALBERTI, *La Arboleda perdida,* p. 189.
[27] C. M. BOWRA, *The Creative Experiment* (London: Macmillan, 1942), p. 222.

y no verte, an elegy Alberti wrote when he learned of the death of a close friend, the bullfighter, Ignacio Sánchez Mejías.

Our fourth chapter shows how, through the use of color, a sense of nostalgia is created in Alberti's post-Civil War poetry. Nostalgia and feelings of regret because of his exile from his beloved «patria» are clearly evident in a number of works but here we shall limit ourselves to *Pleamar, Retorno de lo vivo lejano,* and *Baladas y canciones del Paraná.*

The final chapter is an exegesis of Alberti's book *A la pintura.* This collection of poems on the subject of visual art includes sonnets written in a rigidly classic form on artistic techniques, poems dealing with various artists, and a series of brief poetic impressions on colors «per se». Our conclusion will recapitulate the salient points of each of our chapters and summarize the effective results achieved through the poet's unique implementation of color and other visual techniques in his poetry.

CHAPTER I

Mar y tierra

General observations

One of the central themes in Rafael Alberti's work is the poet's cosmovision, or his attachment, affinity and identification with the elements of nature. Mar y tierra are, for our purpose one of his perpetual sources of inspiration whether considered individually (mar, tierra) or dualistically (mar-tierra). He refutes, as did Juan Ramón Jiménez before him, the possibility of a hierarchy in nature. His poetry conveys, rather, a sense of unity or brotherhood among the elements of nature, in which the poet himself plays a vital role.

> La universalidad del mundo, prístina y original, advierte nuestra hermandad cósmica con la tierra y el cielo, con el fuego y el agua, produciendo la satisfacción de un juego que se realiza en pleno azar y en libertad completa y otorgándonos el divino placer de la omnipotencia.[1]

No where is the feeling of unity among the elements of nature more apparent than in Alberti's poem «Balada de la sinceridad al toque de las ánimas.» The poem reveals his belief that all of the elements of nature are somehow inextricably related:

> Señor, ser viento, Señor.
> Viento, ser campo, Señor.
> Campo, ser yerba, Señor.
> Yerba, ser nido, Señor.
> Nido, ser pluma, Señor.
> Pluma, ser nube, Señor.[2]

His desire to surrender his own human characteristics in order to more closely identify with other forms of nature seems to be omnipresent. In one poem, for example, Alberti tells us that he wishes he had gills so he could join his fiancée who lives in the sea: «Branquias quisiera tener, / porque me quiero casar»(52). On another occasion he asks to be a grain of salt in order that he might remain forever by the sea: « ¡Dejadme ser, salineros, / granito del salinar! »(52).

---

[1] ARTURO RIVAS SAINZ, «Contrapunto y fuga, cuatro compases de Alberti,» *Eos, Revista Jaliscience de Literatura*, Guadalajara (July 1943), p. 38.
[2] RAFAEL ALBERTI, *Poesías completas* (Buenos Aires: Losada, 1961), p. 981. (Hereafter all quotes from Alberti's poems will be taken from this edition. Only the page after each quote will be recorded.)

2

Since Alberti sees the universe as a homogeneous body in which all elements are on an equal plane, it is not uncommon to find in his poetry examples of what Concha Zardoya calls «humanización.»[3] The elements of nature either take on human characteristics or are described in human terms, whether they be fauna and flora or the fish which are to sing along with him: «¡Peces del mar, salid, cantad conmigo!»(26). One poem likens the birds to members of his family: «Señora abubilla, / señor gorrión, / hermana mía calandria, / sobrina del ruiseñor.»(34) «Elegía» presents a skating snail, «patinaba el caracol»(46), and an inquisitive chick pea, «El garbanzo asomaba su nariz»(46). In «Jardín de Miramelinda» and «Rosa-fría,» human characteristics are attributed to a number of fruits and flowers.

The seasons of the year are also personified in Alberti's poetry. The springtime is seen captaining a vessel: «¡Por el mar, la primavera! / ¡A bordo va!»(63). A section of his poem «A Federico García Lorca, poeta de Granada» entitled «Otoño,» depicts autumn as a mysterious figure with gypsy-like features that is seen stabbing the cadaver of summer: «En esta noche, en que el puñal del viento / acuchilla el cadáver del verano, / yo he visto dibujarse en mi aposento / tu rostro oscuro de perfil gitano»(25).

On one occasion the poet alludes to his own song in human terms: «Si mi voz muriera en tierra, / llevadla al nivel del mar / y dejadla en la ribera»(82).

The nucleus of Alberti's anthropomorphic imagery concentrates on the four principal elements of nature, Aristotles primordial common denominators of the universe: earth, water, fire and air. While in this chapter attention is given mainly to «mar y tierra,» it is appropriate to note that all four elements have very definite symbolic connotations in Alberti's poetry. Fire, for example, usually suggests passion, war and surging emotions. Air and water are generally symbols of life and of freedom. Earth may be a symbol of restraint. In «Canción 25» from *Baladas y canciones del Paraná,* the poet appears to be confiding to a friend (the fire) his innermost feelings:

> Cuántas cosas tú me enseñas
> que a veces olvido, fuego. (1027)

Clouds, sky, wind, wings, and other air related elements are personified in the poets work. In one poem he asks the wind to tear off his clothing: «¡Viento, arráncame la ropa!»(80). In another poem the wind is asked to take a message to a sailor to alert him that the lighthouse has no beacon: «¡Corre, ve, viento marero, / y dile a algún marino / que el faro no está encendido!»(79). On at least one occasion the clouds are said to be crying: «Por el mar de la tarde / van las nubes llorando / rojas islas de sangre»(47). Human traits are attributed also to the dawn: «Ya está

---

[3] CONCHA ZARDOYA, «La técnica metafórica albertiana,» in *Poesía española del 98 y del 27* (Madrid: Gredos, 1962), p. 305.

flotando el cuerpo de la aurora»(21). Further references are made to the dawn's «frente»(67), and to its «clara faz»(24). The earth is also personified. In one poem the coastlines indicate a desire for freedom, display their «frentes serpentinas,» and are at once able to speak. They ask a ship's captain to free them from the chains that bind them to the land:

> ... todos los litorales amarrados del mundo, pedimos que nos lleves en el surco profundo de tu nave, a la mar, rotas nuestras cadenas.(23)

The element with which the poet shares the greatest affinity, however, is the sea. Vicente Aleixandre states that this attachment to the sea is natural, «Porque su seseo, su sonrisa agraz, su chispeo clarísimo nacían de lo blanco y verde más gaditanos: espumas y agua del mar.»[4] Alberti's identity and intimacy with the sea lead him to exclaim: «Te reconozco aquí, mar de mi infancia, / hecho a mi propia imagen inocente;»[5] At times the poet suffers a true identity crisis: «¡Qué feliz era, mar! Llegué a creerme / hasta que yo era tú y que me llamaban / ya todos con tu nombre»(537); «Mar, aunque soy hijo tuyo, / quiero decirte: ¡Hija mía! / y llamarte al arrullarte: / Marecita / —madrecita— / ¡marecita de mi sangre! »(53).

In Alberti's poetry the elements are often represented as inseparable dualities, the most common of which is «mar-tierra,» the inspiration for *Marinero en tierra, La amante* and *El alba del alhelí*. Ivan Schulman reminds us that this concept is also central to Spanish romantic poetry and that it is nothing more than an aesthetic representation of the philosophical conviction that the world itself is composed of inherent dualities:

> Expresada en lenguaje simbólico, la polaridad es la equivalencia estética de una convicción filosófica según la cual el mundo está compuesto de dualismos inherentes, que en su lucha por la preponderancia llegan a veces a reconciliarse a favor de elementos más nobles.[6]

But Pedro Salinas is more specific when he states that in *Marinero en tierra*:

> El poeta se considera como «un desenterrado del mar,» como un expatriado que desde la ciudad, que no ve el mar, le sueña y le acaricia, evocándole. Cuando va por las calles de la tierra con el traje marinero que ha pedido que le ponga su madre, camina sobre la ilusión de ir por las calles del mar. En sus aguas ve asomar la primavera; por ellas vislumbra un inverosímil toro azul y oye en ellas pregones submarinos; . . . Este libro constituye como

---

[4] VICENTE ALEIXANDRE, «Rafael Alberti, pintor,» *El Nacional* (July 18, 1957). No page number.
[5] RAFAEL ALBERTI, *Libro del mar* (Barcelona: Ed. Lumen, 1968), p. 6.
[6] IVAN SCHULMAN, *Símbolo y color en la obra de José Martí* (Madrid: Gredos, 1968), p. 82.

un sartal de cantares marineros transfundidos a la tonalidad común de esta primera época de refinación culto. . . . [En *La amante* tenemos] un breve itinerario lírico de su viaje desde Madrid a la costa norte de España. Según va cruzando tierras se le prenden en la retina imágenes de gentes: un cazador, un carretero, una abuela entre sus gallinas; de animales: la vaca en el prado, la mula carrera, o de árboles y plantas: el chopo, la zarza. Imágenes que sujeta y condensa en anotaciones líricas donde el realismo geográfico se sutiliza en idealización de cantar. Aun aquí sigue el poeta con su obsesión marinera.[7]

> Castilla tiene castillos,
> pero no tiene una mar.(104)

In *El alba del alhelí,* the correlation between the sea and the poet's mood becomes even more obvious. The farther removed from the sea, and the longer he remains away, the more disillusioned the poet becomes. Throughout the work there are strong indications that the poet feels out of his element. In «La Húngara.» for example, he is intrigued by the colorful world of the gypsies but fails to relate to it. The poet's more somber mood brought about by his separation from the sea is reflected in the gradual introduction of darker shades of color.

Before treating specific works and focusing our attention on color, a brief summary of some general observations seems in order. While all of nature, with its infinite spectacles, vignettes and moods appears to provide poetic resources for Alberti's lyre, the «mar gaditano» plays a more predominant role. Here «mar-tierra» serves as the playground of fantasy upon which the alternating poet-child or child-poet is playing a series of games of hide-and-seek. On land he is the perpetual, adventurous sailor. On the sea, he longs for the affinity of the shore. There are no vast magnitudes or expanses desired on this «vaivén» of land-sea or sea-land. On the contrary, there is a procession of desires and images that are colorful and gracious. So the crayons move upon this drawing canvas and a variety of activities, experiences and longings are imagined and depicted. The colors of nature, real, re-blended and at times given new hues, are used to characterize or to create fresh images of objects.

While in art, the colors are generally divided into two categories, warm colors or «colores xánticos» and cold colors or «colores ciánicos,» for our purpose, we must re-dispose them, and not treat them as Concha Zardoya attempts to do in her article, «La técnica metafórica albertiana.» The color white, for example, is considered in art a warm color. But in Alberti's images white generally suggests coldness: «velas nevadas,» «heladas terrazas,» «luna nevada,» etc. In art, green is also considered a warm color, yet in Alberti's poetry we find images such as the following: «los cabellos finos / y verdes de tu álgida melena.»(22) Black, on the

---

[7] Pedro Salinas, «La poesía de Rafael Alberti,» in *Literatura española del siglo XX* (Madrid: Alianza, 1970), pp. 187-188.

other hand, which is considered a cold color, is very often mentioned along with red in images of fire:

> ¡Ardiendo está todo el mar!
> Boyeros del mar decían:
> —Bueyes rojos, raudas sombras
> ya oscuro, ¿hacia dónde irían?(63)

Seldom in Alberti's poetry is there an isolated mention of one particular color in a given image. Instead, there appear color patterns, a number of gradations or hues of one particular color, modification of colors through the use of adjectives, colors suggested by images and finally color references which may appeal to other senses as well as the sense of sight.

El juego infantil

In 1925 Rafael Alberti was awarded the Premio Nacional de Literatura for his first book of poems, *Marinero en tierra*. Upon submitting his vote, Antonio Machado, then a member of the selecting committee, said about the book, «Es a mi juicio, el mejor libro de poesía presentado al concurso.»[8] *Marinero en tierra* also impressed Juan Ramón Jiménez and he wrote Alberti a letter praising his first literary effort. The letter has since appeared as a preface to the book.

One of the reasons for the book's popularity was its simplicity and candor. Alberti wrote this collection of poems while he was living in Madrid, but the subject matter deals specifically with the poet's recollections of Puerto de Santa María where he was born and raised. *Marinero en tierra* is not, however, a realistic account of life in the small fishing village. Alberti makes a conscious attempt to see things through the eyes of a child. Hence, commonplace reality suffers dramatic transformations. Puerto de Santa María becomes, as Solita Salinas de Marichal points out, a kind of mythical paradise or world of fantasy.[9] Alberti's descriptions remind us somewhat of Coleridge's descriptions of Alora. Both are depicted as regions of light where there is no darkness:

> Allí nada es oscuro. Todo se corta y se dibuja como arañado contra el aire por una espada diamantina.[10]

The poet-child is unable to distinguish the limits which separate the opposing worlds of land and sea, and confuses the two in his mind.

> La originalidad de Alberti consiste en trasladar el vergel andaluz al fondo del mar de su costa sudeste. Y sobre todo en lograr que, en el traslado

---

[8] RAFAEL ALBERTI, *La Arboleda perdida*, pp. 205-206.
[9] SOLITA SALINAS DE MARICHAL, «Los paraísos perdidos,» *Insula*, 198 (May 1963), p. 10.
[10] RAFAEL ALBERTI, «Don Manuel de Falla,» *Tiempo* (Feb. 10, 1952). No page given.

al nuevo elemento, no se pierda nada de la frescura y alegría del mundo naciente.[11]

As a result, the everyday activities of the small coastal town are often seen superimposed on an undersea environment, and visa-versa. Alberti's childhood sweetheart becomes «la sirena del mar.» The peddler sells his wears from a cart drawn by salmon. The seamstress of the sea repairs the snowwhite sails of a ship. Mermaids cut their hair and mingle with the sailors in the bars.

The predominant tone of the book is one of playfulness and innocence. Alberti had a happy childhood and relives it through this work.

> El jugueteo infantil... a través de una microvisión del mundo... encubre una añoranza de la infancia perdida y el deseo de revivir su inocencia.[12]

This sense of playfulness is achieved through the style and content of the poems as well as through the poet's choice of colors. Throughout the book one senses the presence of the artist at work, lyrically recreating a childhood paradise through a network of chromatic images.

Rafael Alberti's conception of the sea is quite romantic. Some critics have compared him to Garcilaso and point out that the Virgilian idea of an aquatic paradise is present in the works of both of these poets. We agree with Solita Salinas de Marichal that Alberti is not satisfied with merely contemplating the beauty of the sea, but sees it rather as a vehicle for adventure: «Parece invitar al viaje con un ímpetu exclamativo y alegre.»[13] Were we to draw any comparison between Alberti and other poets, we would have to say that he appears to have much more in common with Gil Vicente or even Baudelaire, in whose poetry the sea is highly romanticized and is seen as a possible conquest for mankind.

The predominant colors of *Marinero en tierra* are, the colors of the sea: white, blue and green:

> De blanco, azul y verde,
> vuelve y se va.(75)

What is most interesting is not the colors themselves, but the way in which they are used. We usually find them in images that would most likely appeal to the imagination of a child.

The color blue is most often seen in references to water or in water-related images. The color itself seems to hold a certain romantic appeal to the child. As a child, Alberti frequently saw the sailors in their blue uniforms returning from the sea and associated this with the stories he had read of the famous adventures of the Conde Arnaldos. Would that he could become «capitán de navío»:

---

[11] SOLITA SALINAS DE MARICHAL, *El mundo poético de Rafael Alberti* (Madrid: Gredos, 1968), pp. 68-69.
[12] CONCHA ZARDOYA, «La técnica metafórica albertiana,» p. 336.
[13] SOLITA SALINAS DE MARICHAL, *El mundo poético...*, p. 43.

Madre, vísteme a la usanza
de las tierras marineras:
el pantalón de campana,
la blusa azul ultramar,
y la cinta milagrera.(71)

In another poem Alberti alludes to the sailor suit he wore as a child:

¡Ay mi blusa marinera!
Siempre me la inflaba el viento
al divisar la escollera.(51)

The romantic idea of someday being a sea captain is evident also in the following verse in which the waves of the sea are transformed by the child's imagination into blue castle walls approaching the Spanish coast from Africa:

Murallas azules, olas,
del Africa, van y vienen.(76)

In a somewhat more complex image, the poet suggests that the sea derives its color from the blue bathing suit of a young girl:

Vestida, en tu bañador
azul, hundirás el agua
y saldrás desnuda, amor.(59).

The child's fascination with animals is implied by the number of images in which the sea is compared to an animal of some type. Some of these images are purely visual as in the verse, «¡Un toro azul por el agua!»(72). Other images have a certain emotive appeal. In the poem «Día de amor y bonanza,» for example, the sea is described as a, «loba de espuma azul»(68). The image appeals not only to the reader's visual sense but to the auditory sense as well. The howl of the she-wolf, to which he indirectly alludes, suggests a forboding sea. In the child's mind the sea also becomes a galloping horse: «¡Quién cabalgara el caballo / de espuma azul de la mar»(80). Rivers and canals as well as the sea are described in animal terms. The thinness of the canal is emphasized in this verse from «Geografía física,» in which it is likened as a blue eel: «La anguila azul del canal / enlaza las dos bahías.»(45). In a similar image, a river is presented as a thin blue sword: «frente al sable azul del río.»(40).

In *Marinero en tierra* there appears to be a fusion of the elements land and sea. The sea serves as a mirror which reflects the world around it and which often transforms it. This concept is studied in some detail by Gaston Bachelard in his book, *L'eau et les Rêves*. The author says «L'eau ainsi est le regard de la terre, son appareil à regarder le temps.»[14] Solita Salinas de Marichal applies Bachelard's concept to Alberti's poetry when she points out that the undersea world of *Marinero en tierra* could

---

[14] GASTON BACHELARD, *L'eau et les Rêves* (Paris: Librairie José Corti, 1960), p. 45.

23

be described as the green reflection of the vegetation which grows alongside the water. Hence, the color green, which is generally associated with land, is very often found in images describing the sea.

The relationship between land and sea is most clear in this image from «La sirena del campo»: «tus trenzas de perejil / se te enredan por la yerba.»(32). The image «trenzas de perejil» is a reference to the green of the water, which is often compared to undulating hair in Alberti's poetry. In this respect not only the elements, land and sea, are brought together, but also human touches are added.

The opposite is also true. Frequently Alberti uses water images in describing the vegetation of the land. In one poem he alludes to the «verde lluvia de los sauces»(32). In a similar reference the willows are described as «verdes sauces llorones»(31).

The concept of the sea as a mirror, which reflects as well as transforms reality, is best seen in Alberti's use of light. The reflection of light on the water is visually depicted by the color green. In describing the lighthouse, he alludes to the «faro verde,» a reference to the beam of light from the lighthouse and not to the lighthouse itself. The difference in the appearance of light on land and on the water is clearly illustrated in the following verse:

> El faro verde de Cádiz,
> le raya de añil la arena.(77)

The light, which is green on the water, appears blue on the sand. A similar example is Alberti's description of the moon as a «verde caracol»(66). By using the color green, the poet makes it perfectly clear that he is not referring to the moon in the sky, but rather to the moon's reflection on the water. By associating the moon with an aquatic creature (the snail) the image is reinforced.

The association of the color green with light is revealed in yet another way. The light of the dawn gives the sea its green appearance. In the poem «Día de tribulación» we note the change in the color of the sea with the rising of the sun: «y la mar negra verde pronto sea»(68). In another poem Alberti describes the thin ribbon of light on the horizon at dawn as a green serpent: «Por el alba, / un verde aspidistra clara»(74). In «Cruz de viento» the sun rising over the sea is described as a golden figure riding atop a green crocodile:

> Dorada, clara de oro,
> flora de los fuegos, tú,
> sobre un cocodrilo verde.(55)

The majority of the descriptions of the sea in which the color green is used are purely visual: «¡Más verde es la mar de enero!»(56). Occasionally, however, green has symbolic connotations. The traditional association of this color with life is seen in, «Al mar de nuestra vida, ya / esmeralda y sereno»(24). Sometimes it appears as if the color has symbolic value when, in reality, it is purely visual. In the following verse, for example, the child's imagination associates the color of the sea to bitter mint. Despite the use of the adjective «amarga» there is no symbolic meaning intended: « ¡A las Antillas me voy / por unas mares de menta / amarga»(48).

There are, very few images in which the color green is used in reference to the land. Like the color blue, it is most often associated with water. One of the few applications to land is the description of the Canary Islands as «verdes cañoneros»(24). This image is again typical of the child's romantic fantasies.

Green is also the favorite color of a number of childhood lullabies which we find in *Marinero en tierra*. In one of these lullabies the Nana coaxes the child to sleep by painting for him mental pictures. If he goes to sleep, he will see visions of almond groves and stars of mint. If he does not, the hawk and the night owl will haunt him. In this antithetically constructed image, the color green is generally associated with all that is good. The color black, which is not mentioned directly but alluded to in the poet's choice of images, is associated with evil.

> Cuando te duermas:
> ¡Al almendro, mi niño,
> y a la estrella de menta!
>
> ¡Si no duermes, al monte!
> Vienen el búho
> y el gavilán del bosque.(37)

In another lullaby the poet playfully suggests that the turtle derives its color from eating parsley and lettuce:

> Verde, lenta, la tortuga.
> ¡Ya se comió el perejil,
> la hojita de la lechuga!(38)

The most popular color of *Marinero en tierra* is white. In many of Alberti's images, white retains its traditional connotation of innocence and purity. In the lullabies it is used, like green, to suggest something pleasant: «La cabra te va a traer / un cabritillo de nieve»(38). The poem «Blanca-nieve,» conveys the feelings of innocence and purity. In this composition the subject is a young girl. Alberti uses images like the flower and the melting snow to emphasize both the paleness of the girl's skin as well as her innocence:

> Blanca-nieve, flor del norte,
> se fue al mar del mediodía,
> para su cuerpo bañar.
> ¡Se habrá derretido ya! (62)

A similar mood is expressed in the poem «La niña del mar» where the girl's innocence is reflected in the whiteness of her skirt. There are moral overtones, but they are deemphasized by the playful nature of the poem:

«¡Qué blanca lleva la falda / la niña que se va al mar!»(69). Once again the antithetical structure of the poem becomes obvious when a new element is introduced: «¡No se la manche / la tinta del calamar!»(69).

Alberti's reference to the stars as «blancas doncellas desnudas»(66) in poem # 32 is another interesting application of the color white. The color is directly mentioned in the image as well as implied in the adjetive «desnuda».

In *Marinero en tierra* white is most often used either in images of light or in images of coldness. References to the light of the dawn are perhaps the most common: «y clarea / la alba luz sobre el llanto de los mares»(60). In another verse, the dawn is personified, and reference is made to its clear complexion: «la clara faz del alba, su voz hecha corneta / de cristal largo y fino»(24). White is also used very effectively in some images to suggest coldness. The description of the girl in «Blanca-nieve,» mentioned earlier, is one example of this particular use of the color white. In the poem «Cruz de viento» similar images refer to a young girl:

> Nevada, clara de nieve,
> flor de los témpanos, tú,
> sobre una corza marina.(55)

Ever since he was a child, Alberti had a genuine interest in geography. The polar regions were especially fascinating to him. Throughout *Marinero en tierra* there are numerous references to these regions of snow and ice. In the poem «Jardinero» we find the following image:

> Vete al jardín de los mares
> y plántate un madroñero
> bajo los yelos polares.(40)

In «Sueño del marinero» Alberti refers to the «Gélidos desposorios submarinos»(22).

Occasionally both qualities, light and coldness, are expressed in the same image. The poem «Rosa-fría» which abounds in images of this nature, is a description of a girl ice-skating. The entire picture is one of whiteness: the air that surrounds her, the light in which she is enveloped, and the ice she is skating on.

> Un silencio escarchado te rodea,
> destejido en la luz de sus fanales
> mientras vas el cristal resquebrajando.(28)

Another example of an image which expresses both qualities, light and coldness, is «luna fría» which is repeated various times throughout the book including this verse from «Sueño del marinero»:

> sueño en ser almirante de navío,
> para partir el lomo de los mares
> al sol ardiente y a la luna fría.(21)

Two other colors found in *Marinero en tierra,* black and red, are used in such a way that they do not destroy the overall mood of playfulness and innocence. Red, which suggests passion and is traditionally associated with fire and blood, retains that connotation to a certain extent. However, more emphasis is placed on the descriptive quality of the color and not so much on its symbolic capacity. In the poem «A Federico García Lorca,» for example, Alberti uses the word «sangre» in describing the color of the landscape: «Alfanjes de los ríos, / tintos en sangre pura de las flores»(25). In «Sueño del marinero» red describes a hot summer day: «¡Oh estío tropical, rojo abrasado!»(21). Red is usually accompanied by another color in Alberti's images. It combines with white in a number of mildly sexual images. The description of «Ardiente-y-fría,» for example, has certain sexual overtones: «Ardiente-y-fría —clavel / herido del mediodía—, / desnuda, en la sastrería.»(47). Red and black are used together in order to capture the fiery mood of the poem «Mala ráfaga.» Again Alberti resorts to the use of animal imagery in portraying the drama and movement of a stormy sea:

> ¡Ardiendo está todo el mar!
> Boyeros del mar decían:
> —Bueyes rojos, raudas sombras
> ya oscuro, ¿hacia dónde irían?(63)

Black is used by itself in relatively few images. The traditional connotation of death which the color possesses does not come through very strongly in Alberti's images. Like red, black is generally used in images of a purely descriptive nature. When not mentioned specifically, the color is alluded to in such words as cueva, luto, sombra, muerto, etc. In «Alba de noche oscura,» for example, we find the following description of the night: «Las puertas del ocaso, ya cerradas, / tapian de luto el campo»(27). An ominous sea is described in the following verse from another poem: «Sol negro. / De una mar, de una mar muerta, / la empujó un mal viento»(75).

When the color black is intended to suggest evil or death, it is usually done in an innocent way. In the lullabies, for example, the suggestive nature of the color black is intended to remind the child that it is bedtime and that evil will befall those children that do not go to sleep. In «Nana del niño malo,» mentioned above, the color black is alluded to in the poet's reference to the nightbirds. In the same poem we find the following highly symbolic, suggestive image which also implies the color black: «Ya en las grutas marinas / ladran sus perros»(37).

In the poem «Grumete» the color black is suggested in the following description of a burial at sea, which, once again recalls the child's romantic visions of the sea: «¡A su tumba, cueva abierta / de los mares!»(72).

The additional colors of yellow, pink and grey are worthy of mention, although they are used in a purely descriptive capacity throughout the book. In «Santoral agreste» the poet asks, «¿Quién rompió las doradas

27

vidrieras del crepúsculo?»)(26). «Alba de noche oscura» offers an unusual description of the dawn. The warming effect of the rising sun is visually depicted by the transition in the color of the sea from silver to gold:

> Sobre la luna inmóvil de un espejo,
> celebra una redonda cofradía
> de verdes pinos, tintos de oro viejo,
> la transfiguración del rey del día.
>
> La plata blanda, ayuna de reflejo,
> muere ya. Del cristal —lámina fría—
> dice la voz del vaho en agonía:
> —Doró mi lengua el sol, ¿de qué me quejo?(27)

The «Nana de negra-flor» tells the child: «Negra-flor, no despiertes, / hasta que el aire / en su corpiño rosa / te haga de encaje»(39). In «Día de tribulación» the sea is described as, «el tumulto gris de los azares»(68).

Notably absent from Alberti's color scheme is orange, unless, of course, we interpret the reference to the fruit trees in the poem «La sirenilla cristiana» as a color reference:

> La sirenilla cristiana,
> gritando su pregonar
> de tarde, noche y mañana.
> ...aaaa!
> ¡De los naranjos del mar!(79)

As we have seen from the number of examples presented, the poet's preference for bright colors such as blue, white, green and red and the way in which these colors are implemented, reflect both the innocence of youth, which is the basic mood Alberti has tried to convey, as well as the extent to which Alberti was infuenced by the sea. The reader is thus projected into a world of make-believe in which all of the poet's childhood fantasies are relived. The concentration of poems dealing with the sea has a direct effect on the overall playful mood of the work. As the influence of the sea becomes less noticeable in Alberti's poetry, a more serious mood develops.

Entre dos mares

La amante is a collection of poems depicting the poet's journey across Castilla to the northern coast of Spain. In this work the sea once again remains the essential element. The land represents, as Solita Salinas de Marichal points out, a mere transition from one sea to another.[15] Throughout the first part of the book, the emphasis is on the «mar gaditana» which

---

[15] Solita Salinas de Marichal, *El mundo poético...*, p. 108.

is an integral part of the poet's being as we have seen in the first part of this chapter. In one poem Alberti tells the landlocked people of Castilla to behold him, for in his eyes and through his poetry, he brings them the sea:

> ¡Castellanos de Castilla,
> nunca habéis visto la mar!
> ¡Alerta, que en estos ojos
> del sur y en este cantar
> yo os traigo toda la mar!
> ¡Miradme, que pasa la mar! (94)

All that the poet sees on his journey, he relates to his native Andalucía. In the following poem, for example, a green pasture reminds him of the sea he left behind:

> La vaca. El verde del prado,
> todavía.
>
> Pronto, el verde de la mar,
> la escama azul del pescado,
> el viento de la bahía
> y el remo para remar.(107)

In the latter part of the book, the emphasis switches over to the Baltic Sea. Alberti's descriptions of the Baltic Sea, as we will attempt to show, are significantly different from his descriptions of the «mar gaditana.» We note a similar change in the overall mood expressed by these poems.

The poet's primary objective, in *La amante* is to bring his poetry to the people. This is achieved in part through his use of popular themes as well as through his use of popular verse forms such as the «cantigas,» the «villancicos,» and the «romances.» The color red, which is the color most often associated with this verse, is equally important in Rafael Alberti's treatment of these traditional themes.

Although the poet's color scheme in *La amante* is akin to that in *Marinero en tierra,* there is a significant difference in the concentration of the colors and in their symbolic value. For instance, in the relatively few poems in which we find the color blue, it is generally associated with the «mar gaditana.» In one poem Alberti refers to it as «Sábana azul, con embozo / de espumas blancas y amenas»(109). In another poem the romantic vision of the sea is recaptured in this image: «Una mar de añil y grande, / mi amor, donde guerrear»(104).

Alberti's descriptions of the Baltic Sea, are considerably different. The allusion to such colors as grey and black in the images describing the industrialized northern coast add a somber note to Alberti's poetry. The snow white sails of the ships, the large blue bull and «la sirena del mar,» images which became familiar in *Marinero en tierra,* are replaced in *La amante* by «gasolinera»(110), «lancha de Capitanía»(110), «lancha vapora»(110), and «agua gris de la ira»(111). The contrast is clearest perhaps

29

in this verse in which the color blue is directly associated with happiness and the color black with sadness:

> Tan alegre el marinero.
> Tan triste, amante, el minero.
> Tan azul el marinero.
> Tan negro, amante, el minero.(110)

The color green is found in images which are similar to those of *Marinero en tierra.* Alberti's referecence to the «verdes erizos del mar»(114) is reminiscent of the image from *Marinero en tierra* describing the sea as a «cocodrilo verde.» His description of a horizon as «la cinta verde del viento»(110) recalls a similar picture of the horizon as a green serpent from his earlier work. In *La amante* there are countless references to the «sirenita verde,» an image used extensively in his previous work. In one poem, for example, the sea is described as a giant comb passing through the mermaid's hair:

> va y viene, amante, tu peine
> por los cabellos, mi vida,
> de una sirenita verde.(116)

A rather unique use of the color green is the image, «Aquí canta la culebra, / le escupe verde el lagarto»(96). The image is an excellent example of what is referred to in Spanish as «desplazamiento calificativo,» or when a characteristic of an object passes from one part of that object to the whole. The application of this technique is particularly evident in the poetry of García Lorca. Alberti's image is very similar to Lorca's image in which the «poeta granadino» refers to the «débil trino amarillo del canario.» In Lorca's image the color of the animal is used in reference to a particular characteristic of the animal: the canary's song. In Alberti's image the trait alluded to is the lizard's habit of thrusting (or projecting) its tongue.

As in *Marinero en tierra,* the color white suggests either coldness or light, and very often these two qualities are expressed in the same image: «Viendo pasar la alba fría»(90). Again the color intimates purity and innocence: «De tu manto bolinero / nazca la aurora, Señora»(111). For the most part, the depictions in which the color white is used are not as well conceived as the delineations of *Marinero en tierra.* In fact, at times the poet finds himself struggling to find the proper image: «Con tu pañuelo de espuma; / no, de luna; / no, de viento»(113).

The color which best characterizes the work and best expresses the poet's mood is red. The overall mood of *La amante* is not one of playfulness and innocence like *Marinero en tierra.* This we have seen already to a certain extent in Alberti's descriptions of the northern coast of Spain. The more serious nature of the poetry, however, is more clearly revealed in those poems in which he composes his own versions of the traditional songs and ballads. The color red is of particular significance in these poems. In a poem adopted from the «romance» which begins «De Salas de los Infantes a...,» the color is used in the description of the brutal slaying of one of the Infantes. The poet, then adds his own touch of sarcasm in the last verse for comic relief.

Al pasar por el Arlanza,
un navajazo de frío
le hirió la flor de la cara.
¡Mi sangre, el amante mío!
¡Se me olvidó mi bufanda! (97)

In the poem «Río rojo» we again sense a feeling of horror in the following description of the river:

Con las lluvias no podré
bañarme en el río, amante,
que viene el cuerpo del agua
herido y envuelto en sangre.(100)

A poem derived from the popular «canción» «Zarza florida» conveys a similar mood through images in which the color red is not directly mentioned, but implied:

Hallé tu cinta prendida,
y más allá, mi querida,
te encontré muy mal herida
bajo del rosal, mi vida.(90)

In the following verse the color red is used in drawing a comparison between a young girl and a rose. The sexual overtones of Alberti's images are obvious:

La hortelana más garrida
y la rosa más florida.
¡Mírala qué colorida!
¡Quién le pudiera injertar
su sangre, vida, su herida,
en un caracol de mar! (106)

As we have shown, the colors Alberti employs in *La amante* are similar to the colors of *Marinero en tierra*. The number of references to blue, white and green however are considerably fewer than in his previous work. The greater concentration of colors such as grey, black and red, and the suggestive nature of the images in which these colors are found, are the most significant differences between the two works. The playfulness of *Marinero en tierra,* which is recreated in some of the poems of *La amante,* gradually gives way to more somber, and, at times, even frightening moods expressed in many of the poems.

Cante hondo albertiano

El alba del alhelí is a veritable «cante hondo.» The poems included here are expressions of the land, its traditions, its joys and its sorrows. More than ever Alberti draws his themes from popular poetry of the traditional type: the «jarchas,» «romances,» «cantigas,» «villancicos» and «serranillas.» «Como bien ha observado Juan Chabás,» states Emilia Zuleta, «algunas composiciones de este libro son verdaderas serranillas, diálogos de amor y requiebros entre pastor y pastora en un escenario rústico.»[16] It is true that some of the poems are bucolic in nature; but what makes *El alba del alhelí* one of Alberti's most interesting collection of poems is that all aspects of the Andalusian culture are explored in the work, not just the rustic aspect. A wide variety of themes are introduced: love, death, persecution and a sense of aimless wandering.

The poems themselves are more dramatic. The frivolous tone which characterized his earlier work all but disappears. The mood of *El alba del alhelí,* while it varies from one poem to the next, is considerably more serious. The compositions now offer a much greater range of colors than his two previous works. Poems such as Alberti's «Pregón,» are filled with an array of bright colors and beautiful images.

The poem is an extended metaphor constructed around the image of a balloonvender. The colors of the balloons are clear images describing the landscape and other elements of nature: red cherries, pink and purple clouds, golden sunsets, a yellow sun clinging to the green branches of a celestial plum tree, snow and fire. The element synaesthesia is introduced in the poet's suggestion that the song of the town crier also has a color associated with it.

> ¡Vendo nubes de colores,
> las redondas, coloradas,
> para endulzar los calores!
>
> ¡Vendo los cirros morados
> y rosas, las alboradas,
> los crepúsculos dorados!
>
> ¡El amarillo lucero,
> cogido a la verde rama
> del celeste duraznero!
>
> ¡Vendo la nieve, la llama
> y el canto del pregonero! (149)

The parallel construction of the popular poems lends itself extremely well to the use of color. In the poem «Al puente de la golondrina,» the transition from morning to evening is described through parallel construction of color images. From the poem itself we get an idea of the more

---

[16] EMILIA DE ZULETA, *Cinco poetas españoles* (Madrid: Gredos, 1971), p. 309.

complex nature of the poetry of *El alba del alhelí*. Although the poem is written in the very simple traditional style, the associations drawn are quite intricate. The «estribillo,» « ¡Vente, rondaflor, al puente / de la golondrina, amor!,» is repeated three times in the poem. Each time it is accompanied by a greeting which suggests the time of day: «Buenos días,» «Buenas tardes,» «Buenas noches.» Finally each of the greetings is associated with a particular stage in the creation of a tapestry: sewing, embroidering and contemplating the finished product. The colors of the day are intricately woven into the pattern through references to various flowers.

> —¡Vente, rondaflor, al puente
> de la golondrina, amor!
>
> —¡Buenos días, hiladora
> del agua-rosa-naciente!
>
> —¡Buenos días, rondaflor!
>
> —¡Vente, rondaflor, al puente
> de la golondrina, amor!
>
> —¡Buenas tardes, bordadora
> del agua-clavel-poniente!
>
> —¡Buenas tardes, rondaflor!
>
> —¡Vente, rondaflor, al puente
> de la golondrina, amor!
>
> —¡Buenas noches, veladora
> del agua-dalia-durmiente!
>
> —¡Buenas noches, rondaflor! (147)

El alba del alhelí is divided into three sections, each categorized by a particular color. The first section, «El blanco alhelí,» as implied by the title, includes poems in which the color white plays an important role. Even the names of the compositions reflect the extent to which Alberti has employed the color: «La virgen tú,...» «El ángel confitero,» «El farolero y su novia,» «La calera,» etc. The second section, «El negro alhelí,» which was to have been originally called «Cales negras» deals with all that is tragic and mysterious in life. Some of the traditional folklore themes treated in this section are «La maldecida,» «La encerrada» and «El prisionero.» The poems of the third section, «El verde alhelí,» are of a pastoral nature. The bucolic mood Alberti tries to create is often lost however because too many unrelated themes are introduced. As we will see, very often one color is responsible in determining the desired mood in each of these sections.

The title «El blanco alhelí,» is easily explained by the number of compositions in which the color white appears. In many poems, such as

«La calera,» it is the only color mentioned or suggested in the entire poem:

> Calera que das la cal,
> píntame de blanco ya.
> Pintado de blanco, yo
> contigo me casaría.
> Casado, te besaría
> la mano que me encaló.(145)

The color is often intimated in a unique way. In «La novia» the colors of the moon and the sun are suggested in images relating to a girl's wardrobe:

> ¿Dónde está mi velo,
> mi vestido blanco,
> mi flor de azahar?...
>
> ¿Dónde mi sortija,
> mi alfiler dorado,
> mi lindo collar?(143)

The predominant mood of «El blanco alhelí» is determined in part by the traditional connotation of the color white. A sense of purity and innocence is revealed in a majority of the poems. There are, for example, a number of poems about the Virgin Mary. In some of these poems the color white is directly associated with the Virgin as in the following verse from «Navidad»: «—¿La Virgen tú, / tan cubiertita de nieve?»(131). Even Alberti's images linked to pragmatic chores, convey a sense of purity and innocence. In «El ángel confitero,» there is no direct mention of color, but an outburst of whiteness pervades the ambience, suggested by the angel, his celestial descent, his garb as a «confitero» and the flour he must handle. «De la gloria, volandero, / baja el ángel confitero»(133).

There are some poems, however, in which the color white suggests something totally different. In «El farolero y su novia,» the color is associated with death. It is written in the form of a dialogue, which is typical of traditional verse. Again the parallel construction of this type of verse lends itself well to color associations. In the first verse, the color white is suggested in a reference to light: «que la luna yo encendí.» In the second verse, the color is associated with coldness: «la más álgida que vi.» In the final verse, both of these qualities are expressed in the same image: «gélida novia lunera.» The overall mood of the poem is one of eeriness, with the exception of the last line where a note of sarcasm is introduced when the girl asks, «¿Te di?»

> —¡Bien puedes amarme aquí,
> que la luna yo encendí,
> tú, por ti, sí, tú, por ti!
>
> —Sí, por mí.

34

—Bien puedes besarme aquí,
faro, farol, farolera,
la más álgida que vi.

—Bueno, sí.

—Bien puedes matarme aquí,
gélida novia lunera
del faro farolerí.

—Ten. ¿Te di?(145)

At times it is difficult to find any continuity of themes in the section
«El blanco alhelí.» Some poems, like «La Húngara,» just seem to be
misplaced. The gypsy therein presented, is an integral part of the Andalusian culture, and deserves to be included in Alberti's «cante hondo»
milieu. But we can find no basis on which to defend its inclusion in
this section. The poem does not convey a sense of purity and innocence,
nor is the color white a significant element there. Instead, the poem
expresses the beauty, mystique and illusiveness of the gypsy woman, and
is replete with colorful images like the following:

Con esa falda encarnada
y esas dos rosas de lino
en tus zapatitos verdes,
dime, di, ¿de dónde vienes?(139)

As originally conceived, El alba del alhelí was to have been a collection
of poems expressing the tragedy and mystery which are a part of Andalucía's cultural heritage: the so-called «pena negra andaluza.» The title
Alberti originally chose for the work was Cales negras. The concept of
the book, however, was expanded to include a wide variety of cultural
themes, some tragic and some not. Nevertheless, one section of El alba
del alhelí entitled «El negro alhelí» is dedicated entirely to the presentation
of the more tragic side of the Andalusian culture:

Así como en esta serie de poemas se introduce una dimensión más trágica,
más honda y amarga de Andalucía, que antes no aparecía en la poesía de
Alberti.[17]

The poems in this section examine a variety of personalities who
represent a cross-section of the recondite segment of Andalusian society.
The first poem, «La mal cristiana,» focuses on the social stigma of a
woman who fails to fulfill her religious obligations. «La maldecida» is
about a woman who, because of her clandestine social activities, is the
object of the town's gossip. «La encerrada» is concerned with a young
girl who is forcibly shut in by her parents in their attempt to protect her
honor. «El prisionero» relates the futility of a man whose existence is
defined by the four walls of his prison cell. «El extranjero» examines
the desperate situation of a man seeking food and shelter in a land that

---

[17] EMILIA DE ZULETA, Cinco poetas..., p. 312.

is foreign to him. «Alguien» looks at the mystery which surrounds violent crimes. The color most often associated with each of these characters is black. Other colors are used primarily as elements of contrast.

The suggestive force of the color black is perhaps most obvious in the poem «La maldecida.» The clandestine nature of the girl's activities is emphasized through continual references to nighttime and darkness:

> —Que tú, por la puerta falsa,
> abres de noche a tu amiga
> que, mal amor, es tu amante.(156)

The mental picture the poet has formulated of her is that of a pathetic figure enveloped in darkness and mystery.

> Que quiero verte muy seria,
> que quiero verte siempre muy pálida,
> que quiero verte siempre llorando,
> que quiero verte siempre enlutada.(156-57)

She is the very picture of death:

> De negro, siempre enlutada,
> muerta entre cuatro paredes
> y con un velo en la cara.(155)

Alberti clearly reveals his own feelings about her by describing her as a black lizard and a black crab. In the poem the girl is also associated with such objects as hammers, nails and daggers. Gaston Bachelard reminds us that traditionally references to such minerals as iron and steel generally carry with them negative connotations.[18] They most certainly have a negative connotation in Alberti's poem:

> ¡Vuélvete lagarto negro
> y que te escupan los sapos!
> Porque toda tú eres clavo,
> porque eres martillo y daga,
> ¡vuélvete cangrejo negro
> y que te traguen las aguas!(157)

The poet does not want his image of her destroyed by seeing her well dressed and exuding a sense of false happiness. The manner in which the poet rejects the association of other colors with his preconceived image of the girl strengthens rather than debilitates the overall mood of the poem.

> No quiero, no, que te rías,
> ni que te pintes de azul los ojos,
> ni que te empolves de arroz la cara,
> ni que te pongas la blusa verde,
> ni que te pongas la falda grana.(156)

---

[18] GASTON BACHELARD, *La terre et les rêveries du repos* (Paris: Librairie José Corti, 1948), p. 46.

The poet's feelings about «La encerrada» are considerably different. She inspires the poet's passions as well as his sympathies. Again color is an important factor in the poem. We find allusions to the colors black and red in the following fire-related image expressing the girl's frustrated desires:

> ¿Qué rubí yerve en tus manos
> y quema, negro, tu sábana?(162)

The girl is being kept a prisoner in her own home and remains ignorant of the poet's feelings for her:

> Tu padre
> es el que, dicen, te encierra.
> Tu madre
> es la que guarda la llave.
> Ninguno quiere
> que yo te vea,
> que yo te hable,
> que yo te diga que estoy
> muriéndome por casarme.(157)

The poet pleads with her to rebel and to jump over the garden wall, but to no avail. She is, after all, a victim of her society.

«El prisionero» also inspires the poet's sympathies. In the first poem of the series, he pleads with the jail-keeper to free the prisoner from his cell:

> Carcelera, toma la llave,
> que salga el preso a la calle.
>
> Que vean sus ojos los campos
> y, tras los campos, los mares,
> el sol, la luna y el aire.(165)

The poet's continual use of antithetical elements in the construction of the images is especially effective in dramatizing the prisoner's desperate situation. In the following verse, for example, there are references to iron, a symbol of death and restraint, and to air, a symbol of life and freedom:

> La ventana de la cárcel
> es ventanita de hierro,
> por donde no pasa el aire.(166)

In a similar verse, the use of opposing elements such as «vidrio / hierro» and «sol / sombra» creates a «claroscuro» effect. Those images associated with light, including the glass which allows the sun to shine through, symbolize freedom while the images associated with darkness are symbols of restraint:

> Un corzo blanco que fui...
> Entre cadenas de vidrio
> el sol me amarraba a mí.
>
> Un corzo blanco que soy...
> Entre cadenas de hierro
> la sombra me amarra hoy.(167)

37

In «Alguien» subtitled «Madrugada oscura,» the reader is projected into a phantasmagoric world of horror and uncertainty. The poem concerns itself with the desperate situation of a suspected criminal who returns home mortally wounded only to find that his neighbors and family have turned their backs on him. Black is used effectively in the poem in conveying a sense of persecution and rejection. There are a number of verses in which the color is alluded to through images of blindness. «Cerrados están los ojos / del pueblo»(164), is a reference to the windows of the town which are barred shut. It is also an allusion to the blindness of the townspeople who have closed their eyes to the man's desperate situation. He is rejected even by his lover. The black needle in the following verse is a symbol of that rejection:

> Te entrego mi mano, y tú,
> en su palma dura y tierna,
> le clavas un alfiler
> fino, largo y negro,
> de cabeza negra.(164)

Another image of blindness (large black birds of prey which descend and pluck out his eyes) adds to the feeling of desolation:

> Vinieron, vida, vinieron
> los negros quebrantahuesos
> y me sacaron los ojos.
> ... Y no veía.(164)

In another verse his obsession is described in terms of a dark shadow which follows him around:

> Por aquello que al niño
> en la frente le hice,
> en la sombra no sé
> qué otra sombra me sigue.(164)

While the tragedy and mystery of Andalucía is best expressed in «El negro alhelí» through the poet's use of the color black, red is also used effectively in this respect. One of Alberti's poems derived from a «cantiga de amigo» tells of the violent death of the lover who went to sea. The color red is alluded to in a reference to blood:

> Sobre el olivar,
> sangrando, el amigo
> que se fue a la mar.(170)

In the poem «Llanto del ciervo mal herido» adopted from an old «villancico,» the color red is used in much the same way. In the following image, for example, the color is instrumental in making the association between a flowerstrewn sword and the bloodstained horns of the wounded deer.

> ¡Ay mis espadas floridas
> de anémonas coloradas! (171)

«El verde alhelí» is perhaps the most poorly conceived section of *El alba del alhelí*. Alberti tries unsuccessfully to fuse the pastoral element and the sea; as a result, the pastoral aspect is almost entirely lost. What we have instead is a series of poems very similar in style and content to the poems of *Marinero en tierra*. We again find ourselves in a world of «barcos,» «sirenas,» «marineros,» etc. The mood of these poems, however, is considerably more morbid. Death becomes a common theme:

> Capaz soy yo de matarme.
>
> Si en vida no puedo verte,
> quizás después de la muerte
> pueda contigo casarme.
>
> Capaz soy yo de matarme,
> sirenilla, por tenerte. (192)

The poet's conception of the sea is also slightly different. As in the «cantigas,» the sea in these poems is generally associated with death. The girl awaits a lover who has gone to sea and may never return:

> Triste, se puso a cantar:
>
> —¿Quién me ha partido mi cuerpo
> frente al mar? (183)

The more serious nature of the poems is often the result of a change in the poet's concentration of colors. The most notable change is the absence of the color blue.

A variation in color can radically affect the mood of a poem. In *Marinero en tierra,* for example, Alberti suggests through one of his images that the sea derives its color from the blue bathing suit of a girl bather. In the poem «Fuga» from *El alba del alhelí,* we find a similar image constructed on the basis of an entirely different color. Here Alberti suggests that the sea derives its color, in this case red, from the bleeding feet of a girl walking along the shoreline:

> Descalcica, por las piedras
> ¡Sangrando va!
> Yo, detrás.
> Chinas que eran blancas, chinas
> coloradicas son ya.
> ¡Que se fue!
> ¡Sangrando va!
> ¿Dónde ya?
> Coloradico está el mar. (188)

The mood is also affected by the subjectivity of the verse. Let us compare a few poems from *Marinero en tierra* and from «El verde alhelí.» Because of the objective nature of the verse, the emphasis in the following poem from *Marinero en tierra* is on the descriptive capacity of the color black and not on its symbolic qualities:

> Barco carbonero
> negro el marinero
>
> Negra, en el viento, la vela.
> Negra, por el mar, la estela.
>
> ¡Qué negro su navegar!
>
> La sirena no le quiere.
> El pez espada le hiere.
>
> ¡Negra su vida en la mar! (61)

A more serious mood is created in the poem from «El verde alhelí» by making the references to the color black more personal:

> ¡Barca mía carbonera,
> siempre ennegreciendo el mar! (186)

The same is true of this other poem from «El verde alhelí.»

> Con su sombra en agonía
> mi lindo barco.
> Pena por los mares muertos
> mi lindo barco. (186)

The most notable color in «El verde alhelí» is green, but not to the extent we would imagine. Again, as in *Marinero en tierra,* the color is often associated with light. In the following verse, for example, the light emanating from the lighthouse is described as a green sword:

> —¡Torrero, torrero mío,
> alargue, verde, su espada
> tu faro, por el umbrío
> desierto de la oleada! (194)

In another poem Alberti uses the colors green and white in describing identical scenes at two different times of day. The same shell which appears green in the light of the sun, appears white by moonlight:

> El sol, en las dunas.
> La arena, caliente.
> Busco por la playa
> una concha verde.
> La luna, en las olas.
> La arena, mojada.
> Busco por la orilla
> una concha blanca. (187)

The poet's original intent in «El alba del alhelí» was to fuse the pastoral element and the sea. This is successfully done in the following poem through the use of the color green:

> Por un platanico verde,
> gaviota al platanar.
> —No es verdad.
> El plátano, verde,
> y verdes las olicas de la mar.
> —Es verdad.
> Y luego, al viñedo, verde,
> por un racimico albar.
> —No es verdad.
> El viñedo, verde,
> y verde las olicas de la mar.(185)

Unfortunately, in the majority of the poems the pastoral element is either entirely lost or, at least, overshadowed by Alberti's preoccupation with the sea. In fact, most of Alberti's color references are totally unrelated to the land, which is difficult to comprehend when we consider the nature of the poems throughout the first two sections of the book.

As we have attempted to show, *El alba del alhelí* presents three very different faces of Andalucía; each categorized by a particular color. The poems included in this work are, for the most part, poems of the land. The sea does not play as significant a role in *El alba del alhelí* as it did in Alberti's two previous works, with the exception, perhaps, of the third section. This, in part, accounts for the more serious vein of the work. Alberti's use of traditional verse forms adds a certain dramatic quality to the poetry.

The poems do suffer, however, from a lack of continuity. While white is generally associated with purity and innocence in the poems of «El blanco alhelí,» there are some poems in which the color suggests death. Consequently the mood the poet is attempting to create is weakened. Also Alberti fails in his attempt to fuse the pastoral element and the sea in «El verde alhelí.» Lastly we could mention the fact that there is an occasional poem which appears to be entirely misplaced. In spite of these above deviations, the wide variety of the themes presented in the work and Alberti's skillful implementation of color techniques, make *El alba del alhelí* one of the poet's more enjoyable works.

In summary, it can be said that the duality «mar/tierra» serves as a framework within which Alberti constructs a network of colorful images. There is a direct correlation between these elements and the mood reflected in each of the works. Color also serves as an important element in projecting the mood. The most notable development in Alberti's work, however, is the trend toward subjectivity. The objective nature of the poems of *Marinero en tierra* gradually gives way to a more subjective verse in *El alba del alhelí*. This is a trend which will continue to manifest itself in Alberti's subsequent works.

Chapter II

Aire y fuego

General observations

As we have shown in the first chapter of this study, Alberti's early works, *Marinero en tierra, La amante* and *El alba del alhelí,* are centered around the elements land and sea. While the somewhat less tangible elements, fire and air, are occasionally alluded to in these works, they remain in the background. Beginning with *Cal y canto,* however, we witness a noticeable transition in Alberti's poetry. The water-dominated environment of *Marinero en tierra* gives way to a more ethereal environment governed primarily by the elements fire and air. Solita Salinas de Marichal describes this transition in her book *El mundo poético de Rafael Alberti.* «Se pasa fácilmente,» says the author, «del viaje por las aguas al viaje por el aire. Esta vida siempre abierta hacia el mar en *Marinero en tierra*: El ser mecido (superlativo de felicidad) se convierte en el ser transportado.»[1]

As the elements fire and air suggest, Alberti's poetry beginning with *Cal y canto* and continuing through most of his Civil War poetry is more intense and its very essence more elusive. Lorenzo Varela notes this change in his article «En el aire sonoro de Rafael Alberti»:

> Rafael Alberti confirma en este libro su valor más puro, lo que nosotros sentimos más extraño y de más cercano para comprenderle: el aire sonoro de su poesía. Porque Alberti nunca se nos da en la voz, en el acento, ni en el cuerpo; se nos da en el aire, como un milagro detenido en el viento para nosotros.[2]

The symbolic possibilities of the elements fire and air are far-reaching. Gaston Bachelard reminds us that traditionally the element air is associated with freedom:

> Faut-il souligner en effet que dans le règne de l'imagination l'épithète qu'est le plus proche du substantif «air» c'est l'épithète «libre».[3]

---

[1] SOLITA SALINAS DE MARICHAL, *El mundo poético de Rafael Alberti* (Madrid: Gredos, 1968), p. 222.
[2] LORENZO VARELA, «En el aire sonoro de Rafael Alberti,» *Sol* (April 28, 1936). No page number.
[3] GASTON BACHELARD, *L'air et les songes* (Paris: Librairie José Corti, 1959), p. 15.

In Alberti's poetry when the poet wants to espress freedom, movement or elusiveness he uses such air-related images as wings, sails, birds, clouds, feathers, etc. These images do not necessarily have color associated with them. Instead they very often have a clear and ethereal quality:

> Te invito, sombra, al aire.
> Sombra de veinte siglos,
> a la verdad del aire,
> del aire, aire, aire.(259)

This, says Bachelard, is characteristic of the romantic poets like Holderlin: «Cet éther ne correspond pas à un cinquième élément, il représent simplement l'air tonique et clair chanté sous un nom savant.»[4]. The element air, however, manifests itself in two other more tangible forms in Alberti's work: The sky and the dawn. The images used in describing the sky and the dawn are less symbolic and more descriptive. Color is a significant element in these images. Traditionally the color generally associated with the sky is blue. Gaston Bachelard reminds us that, «Le premier bleu est à jamais le bleu du ciel.»[5] In Alberti's poetry there are innumerable references to the sky in terms of the color blue. In the poem «Oso de mar y tierra» from *Cal y canto,* for example, Alberti speaks of «la larga cola azul del viento»(203). Traditionally the color associated with the dawn is white. This is true also of Alberti's poetry. Throughout his work, especially in *Cal y canto,* the dawn is described by allusions to certain elements in which the color white is inherent. The two elements most often used in this capacity are marble and ice. In the poem «Narciso» the dawn is described as «mármol amante nadador y puro»(207). In «Araceli» we find the following description of the dawn: «No si de arcángel triste ya nevados / los copos, sobre ti, de sus dos velas»(199).

Fire is traditionally a symbol of passion, war and surging emotions. In Alberti's poetry this element encompasses all of this and a great deal more. For instance, it is the only element which has two contradictory connotations. It is both a symbol of violence as well as a symbol of purity. This phenomenon does have literary precedence, however. Gaston Bachelard reminds us that fire shines in heaven and burns in hell.[6] Phillip Wheelright, in his book, *The Burning Fountain,* explains that, «Fire can cause burning pain and destruction; it can also refine and purify.»[7]

There is a wide range of color associated with the element fire in Alberti's poetry. In those images in which the poet wants to emphasize the destructive nature of the element, the colors red and black are used. With images in which fire appears as a purifying element, the colors white and green are used.

The two works in which the elements fire and air are most clearly

---

[4] Ibid., p. 199.
[5] Ibid., p. 197.
[6] GASTON BACHELARD, *La psicoanálisis del fuego* (Madrid: Alianza, 1966), pp. 17-18.
[7] PHILLIP WHEELRIGHT, *The Burning Fountain* (Bloomington, Indiana: Indiana Univ. Press, 1954), p. 306.

manifested are *Cal y canto* and *Sobre los ángeles*. Each of these works will be treated (individually) in this chapter. The first part of the chapter entitled, «Mundo helado, mundo en tormenta,» concerns the first of these works. We will see how the presence of the elements fire and air in *Cal y canto* helps create an atmosphere of chaos and confusion which is further enhanced when presented in contrast to a world of frozen brilliance in which one or both of these elements are notably absent. The second part of this chapter, «Príncipe de luz, príncipe de las tinieblas,» concerns Alberti's most well-known collection of poems, *Sobre los ángeles*. In this work, air and fire ally themselves in a struggle against the world of darkness.

Mundo helado, mundo en tormenta

The publication of *Cal y canto* marks the beginning of an entirely new period in Rafael Alberti's literary career. The poems of this collection are radically different from the simple unassuming poems of his earlier works. The book was written at a time when the relatively new art form of cinematography was at the height of its popularity. By employing images which combined light and movement, Alberti sought to create in his poetry an effect similar to that achieved on the screen. «Perseguiría como un loco,» says the poet, «la belleza idiomática, los más vibrados timbres armoniosos, creando imágenes que, a veces, en un mismo poema, se sucederían con una velocidad cinematográfica.»[8] Alberti tried to achieve this effect within the framework of a highly structured verse. Although there are some poems written in free verse, the majority of the poems of *Cal y canto* are either petrarchan sonnets or rigidly constructed tercets of hendecasyllabic meter.

The influence of Góngora is obvious throughout the work. Alberti employs many of the same poetic techniques used by the «poeta cordobés»: neologisms, hyperboles, hyperbatons, similar images, colors, etc. Alberti even goes as far as to use some of the same structural formulas employed by Góngora. One such formula which Dámaso Alonso refers to as «contraposición de versos» (A si no B, B si no A) is used in a number of Alberti's poems. In «Araceli,» for example, we find verses like the following:

> No si de cisnes sobre ti cuajados,
> del cristal exprimidas carabelas.
> Si de luna sin habla cuando vuelas,
> si de mármoles mudos, deshelados.(199)

An even greater influence than Góngora, perhaps, is the Vanguard movement which was rapidly spreading its influence across Spain at the time. Though the style of Alberti's poems is primarily baroque, the great

---

[8] RAFAEL ALBERTI, *La Arboleda perdida* (Buenos Aires: Compañía Fabril Ed., 1959), p. 239.

majority of his images are ultraist, cubist or futurist in nature. The few poems written in free verse lend themselves very well to the use of images of this type:

> La Torre Eiffel tira un cielo
> de anuncios y telegramas.
> ¡Huye, mar!
> ¡Viva mi nombre en todos los sombreros
> del bulevard!
> ¡Y mi fotografía en bicicleta! (237)

The result of trying to incorporate these images within the framework of a well structured verse, however, is often disturbing. The two prove to be, for the most part, incompatible, as is seen in the following verse from «Guía estival del paraíso»:

> Carreras de los vírgenes cometas
> en cinta, alrededor de los anillos
> saturnales, de alcol las bicicletas.(212)

The poet compares here the movement of the planets to a bicycle race. The overall effect is destroyed, however, since such cinematographic elements as movement and light, strongly suggested by the images, are restricted by the nature of the verse.

Cal y canto was originally going to be called *Pasión y forma*, a title, which, while not as euphonious perhaps as *Cal y canto*, certainly expresses more accurately the nature of the poetry included in the work. The book reflects two diametrically opposed poetic worlds, each of which reveals a unique aspect of Alberti's confused personality.

The reader discovers first a world of architectural elegance and fossilized emotions, which we will call «mundo helado.» It is a world in which the colors white and iceblue reign supreme. Solita Salinas de Marichal describes it as the water-dominated environment of *Marinero en tierra* now in a solidified state.[9] Alberti's images, which convey a sense of coldness and solidity («nieve,» «mármol,» «marfil,» etc.), help create a mood that Robert Ter Horst has described as the «paralytically frozen consciousness of death in process.»[10]

The other world revealed in this work, which we will refer to as «mundo en tormenta» is a world in constant turmoil. Here the images used by the poet evoke force and destruction: «toro desmandado,» «ardiendo,» «vengador,» «can decapitado,» «grietas de sangre,» etc. The predominant colors inferred in these images, red and black, contrast sharply with the frozen brilliance of some of Alberti's other images.

By skillfully manipulating color images, Alberti takes us from one poetic world to another, and, in doing so, reveals two sides of a seemingly schyzophrenic personality: the desire for order and perfection on the one hand, and the passionate urge to destroy on the other.

---

[9] SOLITA SALINAS DE MARICHAL, *El mundo poético...*, p. 160.
[10] ROBERT TER HORST, «The Angelic Prehistory of *Sobre los ángeles*,» *Modern Language Notes*, 81 (1966), p. 186.

There is no logical pattern to the poems of *Cal y canto* as Andrés Sabella would have us believe.[11] Instead, Alberti jumps from one mood to another, sometimes in the same poem, clearly dramatizing his confused though creative state of mind.

Altough the two contradictory moods are not presented to the reader in any logical order, there are certain poems in which each of these moods is clearly defined. We will begin by examining those poems that are most representative of the world we referred to earlier as «mundo helado.» Next we will look at those poems which capture the more intense and dramatic mood of «mundo en tormenta.»

Mundo helado, mundo en relativa calma

The first poem of *Cal y canto*, «Araceli,» is a highly descriptive composition somewhat reminiscent of Góngora. The verse structure, the meter (hendecasyllabic), the use of such poetic techniques as hyperbaton and the correlative as well as the poet's choice of images are all typically baroque. The poem is an analogy between a young woman and the sky. Alberti is not describing a woman of flesh and blood, but rather a woman who is the incarnation of perfection in the classical sense. The comparison between the sky and the woman is achieved through the use of the color white in the poet's metaphors. (Alberti shows a Gongoran preference for such metaphors as «cisne,» «jazmín,» «marfil,» «mármol,» «alba,» «pluma,» «nieve,» «hielo» and «velas»). The color is itself a symbol of beauty, purity and innocence. Each of the metaphors, expresses other qualities as well. Marble, ivory and ice, for example, convey a sense of frozenness or rigidity. Feathers, sails and snow convey a feeling of elusiveness. Thus the woman, like a finely chiseled greek statue, becomes an object of unattainable beauty and perfection that seems to transcend the realm of human emotion.

ARACELI

No si de arcángel triste ya nevados
los copos, sobre ti, de sus dos velas.
Si de serios jazmines, por estelas
de ojos dulces, celestes, resbalados.

No si de cisnes sobre ti cuajados,
del cristal exprimidas carabelas.
Si de luna sin habla cuando vuelas,
si de mármoles mudos, deshelados.

Ara del cielo, dime de qué eres,
si de pluma de arcángel y jazmines,
si de líquido mármol de alba y pluma.

De marfil naces y de marfil mueres,
confinada y florida de jardines
lacustre de dorada y verde espuma.(199)

---

[11] ANDRÉS SABELLA, «La poesía de Rafael Alberti,» *Atenea*, 182 (1940), p. 278.

«Sueño de las tres sirenas» is a highly contrastive poem in which the elements air and sea are diametrically opposed. The poem describes the mermaids' flight from the sea: «las verdes colas de las tres sirenas / que huyendo de la mar y sus pescados»(205), and their escape to the more ethereal environment of the air: «¡Gloria al vapor azul de los licores / y al sonoro cristal de los vasares!»(206).

The antithesis is achieved through Alberti's use of color. The sea is described in terms of the color green, which, in this poem at least has a negative connotation: «¡Qué amarga ya la menta de los mares!»(206). The sky, on the other hand, is described in terms of the colors blue and white. The images used in portraying the sky are appealing, at least in a futurist sense: «automóvil de marfil y plata,» «la resbalada luna azul del yelo,» «un hidroplano de redondo vuelo,» «un patinar de corzas boreales,» «ángeles albos de las neverías,» etc.

SUEÑO DE LAS TRES SIRENAS

Nácares de la luna ya olvidados,
las verdes colas de las tres sirenas,
que huyendo de la mar y sus pescados,

cortas las faldas, cortas las melenas,
reinas del viento, los celestes bares
solicitan en tres hidros alados.

¡Qué amarga ya la menta de los mares!
¡Gloria al vapor azul de los licores
y al sonoro cristal de los vasares!

¡Lejos los submarinos comedores!
¡Honor a los seráficos fruteros
del Paraíso añil de los Amores!

Bajo las ondas, novios marineros,
nunca más, ni por playas y bahías,
los pescadores y carabineros.

Sí por hoteles y confiterías,
alfiler de sol puro en la corbata,
ángeles albos de las neverías.

No en el estío de la mar, regata
de balandros, sino que por el cielo,
un automóvil de marfil y plata,

un hidroplano de redondo vuelo
y, a un patinar de corzas boreales,
la resbalada luna azul del yelo.

Ver cómo en las verbenas siderales,
vírgenes albas, célicos donceles
y flores de los canos santorales,

en calesas de vidrios y claveles,
las ternas van a coronar, equinas,
del giro de los blandos carruseles.

48

No más álgidas ferias submarinas,
ni a las damas jugar con los tritones
o al ajedrez con los guardias marinas.

¡Muerte a la mar con nuestros tres arpones! (205-60)

The poem «Narciso» is an allegory based on the mythological story which tells of a man who, upon seeing his reflection in a pool of water, falls helplessly in love with himself. The Narcissus in Alberti's poem is not a man of flesh and blood, but the sky which, as in «Araceli,» is once again attributed human characteristics. Alberti employs futuristic images in describing the sky as a motorcyclist. The colors of the sky are alluded to in such images as, «chaqueta de sol,» «pantalón de luna,» «alfiler de plata» and «azul motocicleta».

Other descriptions of the sky in the poem are typically gongoran. In one verse, for example, Alberti describes the sky at dawn as, «mármol amante nadador y puro»(207). In another verse he writes: «Lo inmutable, marmóreo y verdadero: / desnudo siempre tú, sobre las aras / de las ondas, besando al marinero»(207). Once again the color white, symbol of purity and beauty, is reflected in these images. The style as well is characteristic of Góngora. The verse which begins, «Y en la pechera, trébol ya de plata...» is a classic example of (a) hyperbaton.

NARCISO

1
(SITUACION)

No en atanor ni estanque, nardo mío,
de metal gualda y perejil crestado,
ni en el florero corredor del río.

A ti, mis ojos, en el agua plana
del mar, te miren, dulces, retratado
y reflejado, arriba, en la mañana.

Náutico el silbo de mi flauta, vira,
golfo rubí en tu nieve persiguiendo,
nivelando la lámina zafira.

No el pantalón de luna y la chaqueta
de sol, ni el alfiler de plata hirviendo,
ni el auto ni la azul motocicleta.

La música del riel y los heridos
montes dispersos, valles y piaras,
para los trenes del verano ardidos.

Lo inmutable, marmóreo y verdadero:
desnudo siempre tú, sobre las aras
de las ondas, besando al marinero.

2
(SUEÑO)

Besando al marinero que te quiere
mármol amante nadador y puro,
que por ti rasga el mar y en ti se muere.

Una boca de sal, despinta y llena
de luz amarga y norte el inseguro
beso que el labio sumergido estrena.

Llora tritón los destrozados ríos
de sus barbas flotantes, relumbrados
de fuego y miel senil sus ojos fríos.

Dos hamadríadas, en el sol internas
las conchas de sus pechos escamados,
el ritmo admiran de las cuatro piernas.

Venus se siente generala y, ciegos,
treinta rayos del mar, combos delfines,
la escuadra en fila arrastran de los griegos.

¡Sal tú, Narciso, que la lunería
te espera, no en el agua, en los jardines
lisos, al sol, de la camisería!

3
(METAMORFOSIS)

Cuellos, puños, lacustres pasadores,
botón de nácar y almidón helado,
las rayadas camisas de colores.

Naraciso, tú, la insignia en el sombrero,
del club alpino, 'sporman', retratado
en el fijo cristal del camisero.

Y en la pechera, trébol ya de plata,
punzando el corazón, sustituídos,
en alfiler, tus miembros, de corbata (207-08)

The poem «Guía estival del paraíso» is similar in style and content to the poems we have been discussing. Again the poet combines Gongoran techniques and futuristic metaphors in describing the sky. The ambiance of the poem is even more bizarre than in the previous poems. The sky here is depicted as a luxury hotel complete with bar, dance hall, game room and gymnasium. The poet, who refers to himself as «San Rafael plumado,» is the «chófer» who, for a cold drink, will take you to this magical paradise.

The images Alberti uses in depicting the sky relate to persons and objects one would expect to find in a resort hotel. Color is very often the only element which allows the reader to visualize these highly complex images. In one verse, for example, the mid-afternoon blue sky streaked

with white clouds is presented as both a richly carpeted marble stairway
and as the rapidly moving keys of a player piano:

> Por una estrella de metal, las olas
> satinan el marfil de las escalas
> áureas de las veloces pianolas.(211)

In another verse the colors of the sky at sunset are revealed in the garb
of an angelic figure. These colors, however, are not mentioned directly,
but are alluded to in the names of drinks one would expect to be served
at a bar:

> ¡Al Bar de los Arcángeles!   De lino
> las cofias de las frentes, y las alas,
> de sidra y plumas de limón y vino.(211)

The sky at night is described as a «campo de aviación» and the stars as
the javelins and discus hurled by gymnasts in a celestial sports palace:

> Y en el Estadio de la Luna, fieros,
> gimnastas de las nieves, se revelan,
> jabalinas y discos, los luceros.(211)

GUIA ESTIVAL DEL PARAISO
(PROGRAMA DE FESTEJOS)

> Hotel de Dios: pulsado por los trenes
> y buques. Parque al sur. Ventiladores.
> Automóviles al mar y los andenes.
>
> San Rafael, plumado, a la Cantina,
> chofer de los colgantes corredores,
> por un sorbete lleva, sin propina.
>
> ¡Al Bar de los Arcángeles!   De lino,
> las cofias de las frentes, y las alas,
> de sidra y plumas de limón y vino.
>
> Por una estrella de metal, las olas
> satinan el marfil de las escalas
> áureas de las veloces pianolas.
>
> ¡Campo de Aviación!   Los serafines,
> la Vía Láctea enarenada, vuelan
> la gran Copa del Viento y los Confines.
>
> Y en el Estadio de la Luna, fieros,
> gimnastas de las nieves, se revelan,
> jabalinas y discos, los luceros.
>
> ¡Reina de las barajas!   Por los lagos
> de Venus, remadora, a los castillos
> del Pim-Pam-Pum de los tres Reyes Magos.
>
> Carreras de los vírgenes cometas
> en cinta, alrededor de los anillos
> saturnales, de alcol las bicicletas.

¡Funicular al Tiro de Bujías!
¡Submarino al Vergel de los Enanos,
y al Naranjal de Alberti, los tranvías!

Hotel de Dios: pulsado por los trenes
y buques. *Hall* al sur. Americanos
refrescos. Auto al mar y los andenes.(211-12)

Once again the elements, air and sea, come into play in the poem
«Romeo y Julieta.» Shakespeare's tragedy is recreated through a series of
rather complex and colorful images, some of a futuristic nature. In the
poem, Romeo is introduced in terms of the air or sky and Juliet in terms
of the sea. The boy's youthfulness as well as his loyalty to Juliet are
expressed through a series of air-related images:

Raudo amor, más ligero que los cines,
que el volar de la azul telegrafía,
pero estático en sí...(215)

Juliet's own fidelity is alluded to by comparing her to a calm sea: «Siempre fija, que yo, de pie, mis ojos, / por ese dócil viso te vela, / darlos
quiero al viaje de tu forma»(214). In some of Alberti's descriptions of
the girl, the sea is mentioned specifically: «¡Oh mar adolescente, mar
desnudo, / con quince lunas cándidas, camino / de los cielos y tierras
ignorados!»(214). The images «con quince lunas cándidas» and «camino
de los cielos y tierras ignorados» are references to the girl's tender age.
In other descriptions of the girl there is no specific mention of the sea.
The analogy would be difficult to visualize were it not for Alberti's use
of color. When Romeo discovers Juliet's body, for example, he envisions
her as a brokendown music box. The silver color of the music box is
the only element which enables us to make the association between the
girl and the sea:

Esqueleto de níquel. Dos gramófonos
de plata, sin aguja, por pulmones.
¡Oh cuerpo de madera, sin latido!(215)

In «Romeo y Julieta» Alberti repeats what he did in «Narciso.» He
plays with the concept of the sky's reflection in the sea. But since each
of the elements in this poem represents a different character, the poet's
images are subject to a wider range of visual as well as symbolic interpretations.

Alberti's use of mirror imagery is most effective in those verses describing
the deaths of the two lovers. Romeo's vision of Juliet as a tomb in the
very first verse of the poem is an obvious omen of their deaths:

Tu forma: ¡qué indolente, qué tranquilo
témpano puro, azul, sueño parado
del agua inmóvil y ovalada —tumba—!(214)

In the final verse of the poem Romeo asks the celestial elements to help
him destroy the image of himself, and in so doing he destroys Juliet as well.

The death of Romeo, who dies by drinking a vial of poison, is alluded to in the phrase «que me ahogo». Juliet's death, who, upon discovering the body of her lover, uses his sword to take her own life, is attributed to the image «daga adversa del viento»:

> ¡Abrid las claraboyas! ¡Rompe, luna,
> daga adversa del viento, que me ahogo,
> romped, herid, matad ese retrato! (216)

Once again the colors of the sky and the sea which are woven into a network of highly complex images, are the basis upon which Alberti composes his own surrealistic version of this classic drama.

ROMEO Y JULIETA

I

(BAÑO)

> Tu forma: ¡qué indolente, qué tranquilo
> témpano puro, azul, sueño parado
> del agua inmóvil y ovalada —tumba—!
>
> Llaves áureas, los grifos templadores,
> que igualaron su sangre con tu cuerpo,
> sin habla ya, sobre tu frente y muslos.
>
> Siempre fija, que yo, de pie, mis ojos,
> por ese dócil viso que te vela,
> darlos quiero al viaje de tu forma.
>
> ¡Oh mar adolescente, mar desnudo,
> con quince lunas cándidas, camino
> de los cielos y tierras ignorados!

II

(FUGA. X. 99.999)

> Precipitada rosa, limpia, abriendo
> con tus hombros el aire... *Las aceras,*
> *saltando atrás, en fila, comprimiendo,*
>
> *tumulto y colorín, multiplicadas,*
> *árboles, transeúntes, vidrieras,*
> *en una doble fuga de fachadas.*
>
> Raudo amor, más ligero que los cines,
> que el volar de la azul telegrafía,
> pero estático en sí... *De los confines*
>
> *de las tierras fugaces, desbocados,*
> *entran los montes y la hidrografía*
> *abrevada de troncos y ganados.*
>
> Ahora que es inminente el atropello
> del sol y que la estrella inevitable
> a lo garzón se corte ya el cabello,

deja a la lengua de los faros, muda,
que entre las sombras se prolongue y hable,
mientras que a ti mi sueño te desnuda.

III
(SUEÑO. FRACASO)

Esqueleto de níquel. Dos gramófonos
de plata, sin aguja, por pulmones.
¡Oh cuerpo de madera, sin latido!

¿Cómo olvidarte a ti, rosa mecánica,
impasible, de pie, bajo el eléctrico
verdor frío, cerrada como un mueble?

¿Cómo olvidar, ¡oh di!, que tu melena,
cuervo sin savia y vida, rodó, triste,
de mi caricia igual, al desengaño?

Sin cabeza, a tus pies, sangra mi sueño.
¿Cómo hacerle subir hasta mi frente,
retornar, flor mecánica, mentira?

¡Abrid las claraboyas!   ¡Rompe, luna,
daga adversa del viento, que me ahogo,
romped, herid, matad ese retrato!

Y dadle cuerda al sol, que se ha fundido.(214-16)

The poem «Invierno postal,» which was no doubt inspired by Vicente Huidobro's «Capitán Cook,» is a description of a picture postcard depicting a winter wonderland: «Tarjeta panorámica: el paseo, / antártico y de azul»(213).   Alluding to one of his favorite images, Alberti in one verse describes the snow as a white bear which has draped itself over the trolley cars: «y el oso blanco abriga los tranvías»(213).   Alberti, curious as to whether or not he has succeeded in capturing the desired mood, jokingly asks his reader, «¿Tiene usted frío?»(213).

INVIERNO POSTAL

Tarjeta panorámica: el paseo,
antártico y de azul. —¿Tiene usted frío?
Sube y baja el invierno en su trineo.

Autorizadas, las peleterías
abren las jaulas del escaparate
y el oso blanco abriga los tranvías.

¡Dadme un beso, románticas señoras!
¡El último, en mi frente sin sombrero,
mis dignas Venus puras, protectoras!

¡Cuidado! ¡A la derecha! Repetida
y al volante, Amarilis, combos rieles
negros dibuja en el asfalto, huida.

¡Caballeros!: el paso a los galanes
que libres de solapa y camiseta
muerte han dado al invierno y sus gabanes.

Rosas del frío frío, descotadas,
por las ágiles pistas de las nieves,
van, andróginas dulces, aurialadas.

¿Dónde os vi yo, nostálgicas postales?
¿En qué cine playero al aire libre
o en qué álbum de buques lineales?(213-14)

Snow and ice imagery is prevalent in a number of other poems as well. The image of the snow as a great white bear, for instance, is repeated in the poem «A Miss X...»: «Temor al oso blanco del invierno»(237). In the poem «Los ángeles albañiles» Alberti describes these angelic creatures using such images as «escayolados de frío»(218) and «astrales blusas de nieve»(218). In «El caballero sonámbulo,» the angel «Pitando va por las nieves, / sin cortar, bandido, el yelo»(231). Finally, in «Carta abierta» Alberti describes the light of the moon using an image highly reminiscent of Lorca: «Un polisón de nieve, blanqueando las sombras»(242).

Mundo en tormenta

There are a number of poems in *Cal y canto* which, though structurally similar to the poems just examined and employing images of an equally plastic nature, evoke an entirely different mood. This is due primarily to the different way in which colors are introduced. The poems we have just examined are characterized by an almost total lack of emotional commitment on the part of the poet himself. Such objects as «mármol,» «pluma,» «hielo,» «hidroplano» and «azul motocicleta,» as well as the colors white, silver and ice-blue, which are inherent in each of these objects, express coldness and elusiveness. In the poems that follow the introduction of more intense colors and the skillful implementation of the elements movement and light in the poet's images, create a more volatile, almost chaotic, atmosphere.

The poem «Busca» is perhaps the most representative of this style of poetry. It is a description of the sea which does not conform to Alberti's earlier work. Here the elements, fire and air, combine to transform the sea into a turbulent and perilous force. Solita Salinas de Marichal describes this phenomenon as the destruction of the sea:

Al viento en su función destructora se une el fuego... Se trata aquí de la destrucción del mar. El viento puede sacar al agua de su quicio, hacerla cambiar de ritmo y movimiento. Pero el fuego acaba con ella.[12]

In the first verse of the poem Alberti describes the sea during a late

---

[12] SOLITA SALINAS DE MARICHAL, *El mundo poético...*, p. 156.

afternoon storm as a stampeding bull. The colors of the sea and the sky are alluded to in such words as «herida» and «ardiendo.»

> Herida, sobre un toro desmandado,
> salta la noche que la mar cimbrea.
> ¿Por dónde tú, si ardiendo en la marea
> va, vengador, mi can decapitado?(199)

In another verse Alberti describes the brightly colored islands as wounds on the surface of the sea: «Se hacen las islas a la mar, abriendo grietas de sangre al hombro de las olas, por restarte a sus armas, muerta o viva»(200).

In «Amaranta» Alberti once again uses fire and air images in capturing the electrified and dynamic mood of the poem. These images are most effective, perhaps, in the following description of loneliness as a mercury-like figure with wings on his heels and passion in his soul who comes between Amaranta and her lover:

> La soledad, dormida en la espesura,
> calza su pie de céfiro y desciende
> del olmo alto al mar de la llanura.
>
> Su cuerpo en sombra, oscuro, se le enciende,
> y gladiadora, como un ascua impura,
> entre Amaranta y su amador se tiende.(201)

The poem «Fuego» is a surrealistic vision of the landscape on a hot summer day. The rocky terrain acquires a seering aspect which could be likened to the hot-white and red metals in a blacksmith's forge:

> Gubias de metal hirviendo
> rojos formones y clavos,
> contra los yunques partidos
> de las piedras, martillando(219)

The sun's bright reflection on the towers is described as splinters of light:

> Astillas clavan las nubes,
> de acero en los campanarios,
> tumbadas torres y agujas,
> antorcha ya los espacios.(219)

The sea, which appears bright yellow from the reflection of the sun's light is described as «mar de azufre»(219). The air settles over the town like a thick heavy cloud:

> Truncos, llagados, caídos.
> nieblas de bulto, los barrios
> hambrientos de gas y voces
> flama las sombras, quemados.(219)

Another black cloud of soot and smoke pushes aside the remaining traces of clear sky:

> El oleaje del humo
> bronco, se encarama al arco,
> pórtico de hollín y yesca
> torcido, del cielo raso.(219)

The mood of the poem is totally pessimistic. There is no relief from the intense heat. The dark sky, usually a sign of rain, is described ironically as a «tromba de ceniza» accentuating the dryness of the atmosphere.

The poem « ¡Eh, los toros! » is a description of an ominous cloud formation accompanied by high winds which announces an approaching storm. Alberti employs a number of images relating to the figure of a bull in his description of the threatening sky. In the following verse, for example, he describes the lightning as green horns and uses the verb «bramar» in reference to the thunder:

> ¡Eh, los toros! Brama el cielo,
> temblando de cuernos verdes,
> de latigazos,. que espantan
> a las estrellas que vienen...(220)

The force of the wind is alluded to in the verse:

> Toros rempujan, sin mando,
> vientos de piedra, que muerden
> muros y sombras de muros...(219)

The following colorful image, a classic example of synaesthesia, best captures the overall mood of fear and horror the poet is trying to convey. The splattering blood is screaming all over the walls:

> Balumba negra, ¿hacia dónde,
> sin rumbo, si nadie duerme,
> si saltando pinta gritos
> la sangre por las paredes?(220)

The poem in which the elements color, movement and light are most effectively employed is «Platko.» It describes the heroics of the Hungarian goalkeeper who played for the visiting Barcelona team in an emotion-filled soccer match against Real San Sebastián. Despite a serious injury during the contest, Platko returns to lead his team to victory. Alberti's poem captures the combative spirit of the game and the determination of the star player who, by his courageous performance, has been immortalized in the minds of many Spaniards.

Alberti projects his reader beyond the realm of reality and into a supernatural world in which the elements air, fire and water all join forces and ally themselves with the goalkeeper in his efforts to defend his goal against the merciless attacks of the opposing team. Platko's supernatural abilities are alluded to by Alberti's references to him as a «pararrayos»(238) and a «tigre ardiendo en la yerba de otro país»(239). From the outset of the contest, however, it appears that even the elements themselves are defenseless against the far superior San Sebastián team:

> Ni el mar,
> que frente a ti saltaba sin poder defenderte.
> Ni la lluvia. Ni el viento, que era el que más
> regía.(238)

With the injury to Platko all hope of winning the contest is lost, and even the elements withdraw their support:

> Volvió su espalda el cielo.
> Camisetas azules y granas flamearon,
> apagadas, sin viento.
> El mar, vueltos los ojos,
> se tumbó y nada dijo.(239)

Even in defeat a supernatural aura surrounds the Hungarian goalkeeper. He is described as a heavenly key which has fallen at the gates of heaven: «Platko, tú, llave rota, / llave áurea caída ante el pórtico áureo»(239).

With the injured Platko's miraculous return, the elements once again come to his aid. In one verse Alberti describes how the air returns to ignite the spark in each of the other ten members of Platko's team inspiring them to victory:

> Fueron
> diez rápidas banderas
> incendiadas, sin freno.
> Fue la vuelta del viento.(239)

The colors of the spectacle come to life in Alberti's poem. The contrast between the bright red and blue uniforms of the Barcelona team and the white uniforms of San Sebastián, for example, is obvious in the following reference to the ultimate defeat of the Donostiarras:

> Azul heroico y grana,
> mandó el aire en las venas.
> Alas, alas celestes y blancas, rotas alas,
> combatidas, sin plumas, encalaron la yerba.(239)

Thus, by combining the elements light, movement and color, Alberti creates an atmosphere of semi-Impressionism and, at the same time, captures the very realistic and dramatic mood of a highly competitive soccer match.

The distinction between the two poetic moods we have discussed is perhaps not as clearly defined in the work as our analysis of the poems suggests. In fact, there are a number of poems in which these two moods are juxtaposed. The best example is Alberti's version of Góngora's «Soledad tercera» included in this collection. The poem tells of a pilgrim who, in his travels, stumbles on to a Virgilian paradise and disturbs the harmony of the environment.

Alberti describes a typical bucolic setting complete with driads and water-nymphs using many of the same highly suggestive adjectives and nouns earlier encountered: «resbaladoras,» «álgidas,» «escarchas,» «marfil,» «azul inmóvil,» etc.

Las célicas escalas, fugitivas,
y al son resbaladoras
de las nocturnas horas,
del verde timbre al despintado y frío,
despiertan de las álgidas, esquivas,
dríadas del rocío,
de la escarcha y relente,
su azul inmóvil, su marfil valiente.(224)

The images describing the chaos and confusion wrought by the presence of the stranger are similar to those we pointed out in our discussion of the second of these poetic moods:

Tanto ajustar quisieron la sortija
del ruedo a la enclavada
del peregrino, fija,
columna temerosa mal centrada,
que, a una señal del viento, el áureo anillo,
veloz, quebrado fue, y un amarillo
de la ira unicornio, desnudada,
orgullo largo y brillo
de su frente, la siempre al norte espada,
chispas los cuatro cascos, y las crines,
de mil leguas eléctrico oleaje,
ciego coral los ojos, el ramaje
rompiendo e incendiando,
raudo, entró declarando
la guerra a los eurítmicos jardines
de las ninfas, que, huidas,
en árboles crecieron convertidas.(225)

The juxtaposition of the two highly contrastive poetic moods in *Cal y canto* is a prelude perhaps to what the reader can expect from Alberti's subsequent work. In *Sobre los ángeles,* there is an even further divergence resulting in the omission all together of bright colors, and the utilization of only black and white.

Príncipe de luz, príncipe de tinieblas

After reading Rafael Alberti's early works from *Marinero en tierra* through *Cal y canto,* one is cognizant of certain noticeable changes in the poet's outlook on life. The innocent and childlike objectivity of *Marinero en tierra,* gradually gives way to a more serious and subjective verse in which the colors take on more symbolic meaning. In *Cal y canto* there is a dramatic breakdown in Alberti's use of color. The refinement and elegance of expression the poet sought to achieve is seen in his concentrated use of such colors as white and ice-blue, while a more or less subconscious desire for chaos is reflected in his use of the colors red and black. Alberti's inability to come to grips with this work leaves him somewhat confused. Shortly after the publication of *Cal y canto*, he returns to Madrid, becomes totally withdrawn and begins searching his soul in an attempt to better understand himself and his work:

> ¿Qué espadazo de sombra me separó casi insensiblemente de la luz, de la forma marmórea de mis poemas inmediatos, del canto aún no lejano de las fuentes populares, de mis barcos, esteros, salinos, para arrojarme en aquel pozo de tinieblas, aquel agujero de oscuridad, en el que bracearía casi un estado agónico, pero violentamente, por encontrar una salida a las superficies habitadas, al puro aire de la vida?[13]

Alberti's dissatisfaction with one collection of poems is certainly not the only explanation for the poet's depression. He undergoes also at this time a series of personal hardships which include a prolonged illness requiring rest and medical attention, financial difficulties, and failure to complete his degree at the University. J. G. Muela believes that Alberti's problems stem from an ill-fated love affair.[14] Whatever the reasons, Alberti discovers a certain introspectiveness he had not experienced previously. The direct tangible result of his soul searching is *Sobre los ángeles*, his best conceived and most artistic work.

Alberti's spiritual crisis is clearly revealed in *Sobre los ángeles*. The poet shows that he is aware of the growing conflict within himself and, like Bécquer, he sees his poetry as a means of freeing his mind from the forces which occupy it. In order to visually represent the crisis, Alberti reduces everything to black and white. *Sobre los ángeles* is devoid of bright colors. The mood is expressed perhaps even more forcefully, however, through a series of antithetical images of light and dark.

Sobre los ángeles is not the first work in which Alberti employs contrasting images of light and dark. We find examples of this as early as *Marinero en tierra*. Even when Alberti used other colors such as red, blue and green for purely descriptive purposes, black and white appeared to have some symbolic connotations, almost always with moral overtones. In the poem «Mi corza» adopted from a «canción popular,» the traditional concept of white and black representing good and evil is readily apparent: «... mi corza blanca. / Los lobos la mataron / al pie del agua»(35).

While black and white are occasionally found in isolated images in *Marinero en tierra*, it is more common to find the two colors juxtaposed. This is particularly true of the poems in which Alberti uses popular verse forms since the parallel construction of the verses lends itself particularly well to the antithetical use of black and white. In verses of this nature, it is not uncommon to find black and white associated with other elements which have more or less the same symbolic connotation. For example,

---

[13] RAFAEL ALBERTI, *La Arboleda perdida*, p. 268.
[14] JOAQUÍN GONZÁLEZ MUELA, «¿Poesía amorosa en *Sobre los ángeles*?,» *Insula*, 80 (August 1952).

white is generally associated with air, water and light, all symbols of life. Black, on the other hand, is a symbol of death and darkness and is most often found in earth related images. The association of black and white with these other elements is especially obvious in the poem «Trenes»:

> Tren del día, detenido
> frente al cardo de la vía.
>
> —Cantinera, niña mía,
> se me queda el corazón
> en tu vaso de agua fría.
>
> Tren de noche, detenido
> frente al sable azul del río.
>
> —Pescador, barquero mío,
> se me queda el corazón
> en tu barco negro y frío.(40)

We do not find the same antithetical use of black and white in *La amante*. Black and white are used individually, however, in a number of the poems. The somber tone of «El Cristo de Burgos» is achieved through Alberti's effective use of the color black:

> Por mis más negros difuntos
> dice. No sé de qué eres,
> Cristo moreno de Burgos,
> no.
>
> —De piel de búfalo dicen,
> dicen que de piel de búfalo,
> yo.(102)

In *El alba del alhelí* there are also relatively few poems in which we find juxtaposed images of black and white. Alberti generally makes a clear distinction between the colors. One of the more obvious indications of this is the division of the work into three sections each characterized by an individual color: «El verde alhelí,» «El blanco anhelí» and «El negro alhelí». «El negro alhelí» captures the pain and anguish which is a part of the religious heritage of the Andalusian people and which is epitomized in the traditional «saeta andaluza». The poet focuses on representative figures of society which reflect in one sense or another this suffering. There are a number of direct references to the color black as well as words and images evoking the color: «enlutada»(155), «muerta»(155), «sombras frías»(155), «noche»(156), «cuervo negro del aire»(157), «cangrejo negro»(157), «martillo»(157), «calabozo oscuro»(167). In «El blanco alhelí» the color white is alluded to in a number of words and images: «nieve»(131), «Confitería»(133), «alba»(131), «luna»(145), «gélida novia lunera»(145), «calera»(145), «cal-y-nieve»(145), «agua-dalia-durmiente»(148). One of the few poems of *El alba del alhelí* in which we do find antithetically constructed images is «La vaca labradora.» The colors again appear to have moral overtones:

> ¡Torrero, torrero mío,
> alargue, verde, su espada
> tu faro, por el umbrío
> desierto de la oleada! (194)

The ray of light from the lighthouse shining over the dark sea is a symbol of spiritual guidance or illumination. Although the color of the light is in this case green and not white, the contrast is equally forceful and the essence of the verse is not lost.

A similar idea is conveyed in poem 8 from «El verde alhelí,» but here the symbol of spiritual guidance is not a ray of light but a white dog captaining a vessel over troubled seas:

> Con su sombra en agonía,
> mi lindo barco.
> Pena por los mares muertos
> mi lindo barco.
> Capitán triste en la proa,
> mi mastín blanco. (186)

Using images of light and dark in the poem «La leona,» two totally different states of mind, happiness and sadness, are described. The colors black and white are suggested in the contrasting images «redes de luto» and «redes de plata»:

> Cantando a la puerta, tú,
> labrando redes de plata...
>
> Llorando a la puerta, tú,
> labrando redes de luto. (190)

Because of the complex nature of the poems of *Cal y canto,* there are again very few poems in which we find antithetically constructed images of light and dark. One exception is, of course, the poem «Claroscuro.» The poem itself is a preview of what we can expect from *Sobre los ángeles.* Many of the elements which make up *Sobre los ángeles* are found on a smaller scale in this poem. The breakdown of reality in terms of good and evil, light and dark, and up and down is clearly evident in «Claroscuro»: «Naufragabas tú abajo en lo hondo oscuro / y yo arriba en lo claro»(221). In this work the colors black and white have very definite moral values assigned to them. In the following verse, for example, the poet sees himself as a symbol of spiritual guidance, a ray of light amidst darkness: «... Y yo —me estabas viendo—, / luz ante el precipicio de las sombras...»(221).

While it is obvious that Alberti was from the beginning conscious of his use of black and white, it is not until *Sobre los ángeles* that there emerges a total breakdown of reality into elements of light and dark. We will see how in this work Alberti explores the full range of possibilities included within the context of a well conceived network of antithetically constructed images.

The structure of Sobre los ángeles, as most critics have pointed out, is essentially vertical. «Asciende y desciende por diversos estratos de su mundo subconsciente.»[15] These same critics, nevertheless, are not in agreement as to whether or not the work itself represents a descension into hell, or an escape upward. Luis Felipe Vivanco sees Alberti's struggle as, «una escapada hacia lo alto partiendo de una situación humana desesperada.»[16] Solita Salinas prefers to describe it as a thwarted attemp at an ascension. «Un esfuerzo hacia arriba y su fracaso.»[17] C. B. Morris, on the other hand, sees it quite differently: «Desde lo alto se desploman sobre el poeta ruinas de catástrofes celestes.»[18] The one thing that the critics do agree on is the fact that the traditional heaven-hell concept is quite apparent in the work. Whether or not Alberti was influenced by San Juan de la Cruz or by Milton with respect to this has no real bearing on the work itself.

Sobre los ángeles is a book of contrasts. The most visually obvious is the contrast between black and white, yet the relationship between these two colors is not necessarily antithetical. There are times in which black and white are employed in a similar capacity. White is generally considered a warm color and black a cold color. When white is associated with heat or light, it has a positive moral value. The word «luz» in Alberti's poetry represents spirituality, purity, beauty, freedom, and life, and is often found in conjunction with other life giving elements such as air and water. It is not uncommon to find white associated also with fire when the poet wants to present fire as a purifying element. The word «sombra,» on the other hand, represents evil, moral depravity and death. There are a number of images in which the color white is used to suggest a static or frozen state of being and thus has a negative connotation. The images «cal» and «nieve» are used in this respect even in Alberti's earlier works. Therefore, while there are references to black and white throughout Sobre los ángeles, the colors are not always presented antithetically.

The «ángeles» referred to in the title of the work are symbolic representations of the conflicting elements within the poet's own subconscious. They do not in any way resemble theological figures just as black and white do not necessarily represent the traditional concepts of good and

---

[15] ALBERTO MONTERDE, «Inquietudes y medievalismo en la poesía de Rafael Alberti,» Universidad de México, 9 (1954), p. 9.

[16] LUIS FELIPE VIVANCO, «Rafael Alberti en su palabra acelerada y vestida de luces,» in Introducción a la poesía española contemporánea (Madrid: Guadarrrama, 1961), p. 236.

[17] SOLITA SALINAS DE MARICHAL, El mundo poético..., p. 219.

[18] C. B. MORRIS, «Las imágenes claves de Sobre los ángeles,» Insula, 198 (May 1963), p. 14.

evil: «... en el mundo de *Sobre los ángeles* no hay conciencia de identidad que permita diferenciar el bien del mal.»[19]

Sobre los ángeles is divided into three parts, each of which is entitled «Huésped de las nieblas,» a title Alberti borrowed from Bécquer. The first «Huésped de las nieblas» describes a conflict between the forces of light and darkness which is taking place within the poet himself, and in which the forces of light find themselves totally defenseless. The struggle continues in the second «Huésped de las nieblas,» but the forces of light now armed with a new weapon, heat, attempt to rise or permeate through the darkness which envelops the poet. In the third «Huésped de las nieblas» Alberti looks back to a time before the crisis and attempts to rationalize what has happened to him. He relates his experiences to the situation of mankind.

Huésped de las nieblas (I)

The first part of *Sobre los ángeles* is perhaps the most difficult to analyze. The poems describe a conflict which is raging within the poet's subconscious mind. Alberti is the helpless victim: «Viento contra viento. / Yo, torre sin mando, en medio»(256). The image of the poet as a besieged fortress is seen repeatedly: «Y se derrumban murallas, / los fuertes de las ciudades / que me velaban»(252). «Llevaba una ciudad dentro. / La perdió. / Le perdieron»(253).

The overall mood of this section of poems is one of futility. The very first poem, «Paraíso perdido» is full of images which convey this mood:

> ... muerta en mí la esperanza,...(248).
>
> ¡Paraíso perdido!
> Perdido por buscarte,
> yo, sin luz para siempre.(248)

The poet's mental and physical state is reflected in a variety of images which describe the poet's feeling of emptiness. The most poignant, perhaps, is the empty house: «Sola. / sin muebles y sin alcobas, / deshabitada»(249). Alberti compares himself also to a black empty sack: «Quedó mi cuerpo vacío, / negro saco, a la ventana»(250). He is an empty pillowcase: «... funda vacía, sola»(254). In some of these references the poet employs what Carlos Bousoño calls the «tú testaferro». In the following verse, for example, he objectively sees himself as a dry well:

> Y tú, muerto,
> tú, una cueva,
> un pozo tú, seco.(254)

---

[19] SOLITA SALINAS DE MARICHAL, «Los paraísos perdidos,» *Insula*, 198 (May 1963), p. 10.

All of the poet's senses appear to be in a state of paralysis. On a number of occasions, he laments the fact that he cannot see or be seen. This spiritual blindness is expressed very clearly in the following verse in which his eyes are pierced by large thorns of forgetfulness:

> De mi corazón, muerta,
> perforando tus ojos.
> Largas púas de encono
> y olvido.(251)

There are allusions as well to a type of spiritual muteness. In the poem «Paraíso perdido,» Alberti is engulfed by an all-encompassing silence:

> ¡Atrás, atrás! ¡Qué espanto
> de tinieblas sin voces!...
> Silencio. Más silencio.
> Inmóviles los pulsos
> del sinfín de la noche.(248)

«El cuerpo deshabitado» appears as crying in the wilderness where desolation is overwhelming: «Grito. / «Nada! / Un boquete, sin eco»(253). The poet's own spiritual vacuum echoes the muteness of his soul: «... mi corazón, sin voz, ni batallones»(255).

A number of perceptions refer to a physical paralysis or sense of inertia that embraces him. Hard, impenetrable elements such as marble mirror this state. The color white, which is evoked through images of this nature, lends itself well to the overall dramatic effect since it contrasts sharply with the all-encompassing darkness suggested in many of the other symbols: « ¡Oh anhelo, fijo mármol, / fija luz, fijas aguas / movibles de mi alma»(255).

While the poet is the obvious victim of the conflict, he appears to have little control over the situation. He tries to ally himself with the forces of light only to realize that he is fighting a losing battle. The forces of light are totally defenseless against the forces of darkness. This seemingly onesided conflict has been appropriately defined by Robert Ter Horst as an «encounter between gutted darkness and impotent light.»[20] In «El ángel de los números» Alberti uses the blackboard image to show the futility of the struggle: «Tizas frías esponjas / rayaban y borraban / la luz de los espacios»(257). The overall feeling of futility is indicated by such words as «muerta» and «fría»: «La luz, muerta en las esquinas / y en las casas»(250). «Fría luz en silencio / de una oculta ventana»(254). And the forces of light finally succumb:

> Ya el fallo de la luz hunde su grito,
> juez de sombra, en tu nada.
> (Y en el mundo una estrella fue apagada.
> Otra en el infinito.) (256)

---

[20] ROBERT TER HORST, «The Angelic...», p. 187.

The battle is over, the poet is lured to the enemies side by a false light, and finally taken prisoner by the forces of darkness: «Cautivo me traes / a tu luz, que no es la mía, / para tornearme»(261). He will not be deceived, however, and continues to resist the darkness even in defeat. The false light suggests to the poet that perhaps he had been misguided all along. He comes to realize that the forces of light were from the very beginning at a disadvantage because they had been confronting darkness in its own domain. Alberti had wrongly associated light with earth-related images («mármol,» «cal,» «tiza,» etc.), when he should have sensed the affinity of light with air. Again the symbolic nature of the elements becomes quite apparent. The earth is described as the domain of death and darkness while the air is the region most often associated with light and hope. The poet, imbued with a new found sense of optimism, challenges the darkness to yet another confrontation, this time on the poet's own terms:

> Te invito, sombra, al aire.
> Sombra de veinte siglos,
> a la verdad del aire,
> del aire, aire, aire.
>
> Sombra que nunca sales
> de tu cueva,...
> Sombra sin luz, minera
> por las profundidades
> de veinte tumbas, veinte
> siglos huecos sin aire...
>
> ¡Sombra, a los picos, sombra,
> de la verdad del aire,
> del aire, aire, aire! (259)

Somehow the forces of light which appeared earlier to be defeated, come to life. This rebirth is symbolically presented in the baptismal ceremony alluded to in the following verse: «La luz moja el pie en el agua»(262). Suddenly there is movement where before there was none: «Gira más de prisa el aire«(262). Where there was muteness suddenly there registers sound: «¡Campanas!»(262). The poet himself experiences a kind of rebirth within:

> Dentro del pecho se abren
> corredores anchos, largos,
> que sorben todas las mares.
>
> Vidrieras,
> que alumbran todas las calles.(261)

Huésped de las nieblas (II)

In the second part of Sobre los ángeles, also entitled «Huésped de las nieblas,» the struggle between light and darkness is renewed. The forces of light now armed with a new weapon, heat, launch a counter assault against the world of darkness. In the poem «Los dos ángeles» Alberti beckons this new angel of light to guide him through the darkness:

> Angel de luz, ardiendo,
> ¡oh ven!, y con tu espada
> incendia los abismos donde yace
> mi subterráneo ángel de las nieblas.(263)

In what Solita Salinas de Marichal refers to as «la prueba del fuego,» the forces of light attempt to dispell the darkness to allow the elements of life to pass through:[21]

> Cinco manos de ceniza,
> quemando la bruma, abriendo
> cinco vías
> para el agua turbia,
> para el turbio viento.(264)

But the forces of light are still unable to penetrate the cloud of darkness which envelops the poet. His senses remain in a state of paralysis:

> Y no viste.
> Era su luz la que cayó primero.
> Mírala, seca, en el suelo.
>
> Y no oíste.
> Era su voz la que alargada hirieron.
> Oyela muda, en el eco.
>
> Y no oliste.
> Era su esencia la que hendió el silencio.
> Huélela fría, en el viento.
>
> Y no gustaste.
> Era su nombre el que rodó deshecho.
> Gústalo en tu lengua, muerto.
>
> Y no tocaste.
> El desaparecido era su cuerpo.
> Tócalo en la nada, yelo.(264)

Many of the same images used to describe the poet's physical and mental state that we saw in the first «Huésped de las nieblas» are repeated here. In «Los ángeles sonámbulos» an all-embracing sense of paranoia is revealed through images of blindness («los ojos invisibles de las alcobas,» «echad la llave para siempre a vuestros párpados,» «ojos invisibles, atacan,» «Ruedan pupilas muertas»), and images of muteness («los oídos invisibles de las alcobas,»«mi boca es un pozo de nombres, / de números y letras difuntos,» «los ecos se hastían sin mis palabras,» «lo que jamás

---

[21] SOLITA SALINAS DE MARICHAL, *El mundo poético...*, p. 245.

dije desprecia y odia al viento,» «Pero oídos se agrandan contra el pecho. / De escayola, fríos, / bajan a la garganta, / a los sótanos lentos de la sangre, / a los tubos de los huesos»(277). Despite the very obvious visual contrast, the colors (black and white) are used in a similar capacity. Both have negative connotations. Black is strongly suggested in the aforementioned images of blindness, and white in such images as «grietas de nieve» and «De escayola, fríos.»

«El ángel de carbón» is quite different. It is perhaps one of the clearest examples of the antithetical construction of color images in *Sobre los ángeles*. Words and images which previously had negative connotations are now seen in a different light. Here «nieve refers of his life, while his present state is described as «carbón» and «sucio»:

> Feo, de hollín y fango.
> ¡No verte!
>
> Antes, de nieve, áureo,
> en trineo por mi alma.
> Cuajados pinos. Pendientes.
>
> Y ahora por las cocheras,
> de carbón, sucio.
> ¡Te lleven! (268)

Alberti's paranoia manifests itself in other ways as well. The poet is continually alluding to the fact that he is being deceived. In «Engaño» this idea is conveyed through yet another reference to blindness: «Alguien detrás, a tu espalda, tapándote los ojos con palabras»(267).

Images of muteness are effectively employed in «El ángel envidioso.» The poet's inability to communicate is projected through images like the tower whose windows are barred and the wasted cities cluttered with dead bodies:

> Leñadoras son, ¡defiéndete!,
> esas silbadoras hachas
> que mueven mi lengua.
>
> Hoces de los vientos malos,
> ¡alerta!,
> que muerden mi alma.
>
> Torre de desconfianza,
> tú.
> Tú, torre del oro, avara.
> Ciega las ventanas.
>
> O no, mira.
>
> Hombres arrasados, fijos,
> por las ciudades taladas.
> Pregúntales.
>
> O no, escucha.(269)

«Los ángeles mudos,» again introduces images of muteness, but this time not in reference to the poet. Alberti appears rather to be making a social comment. He suggests that there is a total lack of communication among people everywhere:

> Inmóviles, clavadas, mudas mujeres de los zaguanes
> y hombres sin voz, lentos, de las bodegas,
> quieren, quisieran, querrían preguntarme...
>
> Y van a morirse, mudos,
> sin saber nada.(273-74)

The overall mood of this second section does not reflect the degree of hopelessness and depression of the first «Huésped de las nieblas.» In «Los ángeles bélicos» from the first «Huésped de las nieblas,» the poet describes the conflict within himself as «viento contra viento.» He is a «torre sin mando.» A similar poem from the second «Huésped de las nieblas,» finds the poet lying motionless, but his soul at least is described as wandering:

> Sur.
> Campo metálico, seco.
> Plano, sin alma, mi cuerpo...
>
> Norte.
> Espiral sola mi alma,
> jaula buscando a su sueño.(270-71)

«Los ángeles de la prisa» offer Alberti «acelerado aire de si sueño»(265); «El alma en pena» portrays a truly «alma en pena, sola, / esa alma en pena siempre perseguida por un resplandor muerto»(274); «El ángel bueno» will make Alberti's soul navigable:

> Para, sin lastimarme,
> cavar una ribera de luz en mi pecho
> y hacerme el alma navegable.(275)

While the poet's soul roams in search of freedom, there are also definite signs of life deep within the poet's body. «El ángel avaro,» for example, transforms the poet's body into a volcano which sooner or later is bound to erupt:

> Temblores subterráneos le sacuden la frente,
> Tumbos de tierra desprendida,
> ecos desvariados,
> sones confusos de piquetas y azadas,
> los oídos.
> Los ojos,
> luces de acetileno,
> húmedas, áureas galerías.
> El corazón,
> explosiones de piedras, júbilos, dinamita.
>
> Sueña con las minas.(276)

Thus the second «Huésped de las nieblas,» like the first, also ends on a somewhat optimistic note.

Huésped de las nieblas (III)

Alberti appears to be in the poems of this third section much more conscious of his use of black and white. Since his color spectrum is limited, the poet relies heavily on these two colors in evoking certain dramatic visual effects and in deriving the essence of some rather abstract images. The verse, «Un maniquí de luto agoniza sobre un nardo»(286), from «Invitación al aire,» for example, is an excellent example of the way in which black and white are employed. The visual quality, as well as the emotional appeal of this image, would be lost were it not for the skillful juxtaposition of black and white within the verse itself. On the one level, the colors are instrumental in achieving the visual comparison between the flower of the spikenard and a woman dressed in black and lying on her death-bed. On another level they serve to emphasize the poet's feelings of pain, anguish and insensitivity to life. The colors also serve to make the antithesis more visual. The color black, which is suggested in the word «luto,» for example, is associated with an object which is artificial (the mannequin) while white is associated with the flower.

There are poems in which the references to black and white are clearly descriptive. This is particularly true of those compositions which do not deal specifically with the poet's emotional crisis. «Los ángeles colegiales,» take Alberti back to his schooldays; the poet refers to «el secreto nocturno de las pizarras»(284), and recalls that «nuestros dedos eran de tinta china»(285). Other poems, especially those relating to the poet's crisis mirror their symbolic connotations, as our analysis of some of these poems will show.

In this section Alberti looks back on his life and attempts to reconstruct the series of events which ultimately led to his emotional crisis. There are strong indications in these poems that it was an ill-fated love affair which triggered the crisis. Alberti addresses himself to a «tú» previously absent in his references. In the following verse from «Los tres recuerdos del cielo,» for example, the «tú» appears to be used in reference to a woman. The verse describes the poet's first encounter with her:

> Cuando tú abriste en la frente sin corona, del cielo,
> la primera dinastía del sueño.
> Cuando tú, al mirarme en la nada,
> inventaste la primera palabra.
> Entonces, nuestro encuentro.(279)

All of the lines devoted to meeting her and the early stages of their relationship are filled with reflections of the poet's happiness. The color white emerges as a most instrumental tool in conveying this happiness, peace and tranquillity: «Paseaba con un dejo de azucena que piensa»(278). In the various references to the girl the color white is used to suggest innocence while a second characteristic, her elusiveness, is introduced by associating her with the element air: «Blanca alumna del aire, temblaba con las estrellas, con la flor y los árboles»(278). «Nieve viva» seems to invest the girl with a white garb all her own. Here Alberti uses metaphors of snow and ice in conveying a sense of innocence and mystique. The poet's own romantic desires are expressed through an antithetically opposed image of fire:

> Sin mentir, ¡qué mentira de nieve anduvo muda por mi sueño!
> Nieve sin voz, quizás de ojos azules, lenta y con cabellos.
> ¿Cuándo la nieve al mirar distraída movió bucles de fuego?(285)

The favorable connotation of the element snow in the above verse seems to be exposed to a new light by Alberti. Snow and ice, earlier, were most often associated with death or paralysis. Yet, the association of these elements with the girl in the verses cited is quite understandable if we consider Alberti's original fascination with the geographical regions of ice and snow. The poem «Expedición» from this same section is a reminder of the poet's childhood fantasies. There are a number of references to Scandinavia in the poem; perhaps the most obvious being:

> No se sabe si el sur emigró al norte o al oeste,
> 10.000 dólares de oro a quien se case con la nieve.
>
> Pero he aquí a Eva Gúndersen.(284)

Thus, while the elements, snow and ice, generally have a negative connotation in Alberti's poetry, there is a viable explanation for their use here in expressing the beauty, innocence and mystique of the girl.

«El ángel de arena» again introduces «tú» in reference to this same girl. The poem relates how the poet was seduced by the girl. Through an extended metaphor he suggests that it was the innocence of the girl's eyes that attracted him to her. The metaphor is constructed around the figure of a young boy who is a symbol of that innocence. A number of associations are made between the boy and the sea, and between the sea and the girl's eyes. The poet briefly considers his freedom (iba a ser ... literal desprendido), but ultimately gives in to his desires (me hundiste en tus ojos).

> Seriamente, en tus ojos era la mar dos niños que me espiaban,
> temerosos de lazos y palabras duras.
> Dos niños de la noche, terribles, expulsados del cielo,
> cuya infancia era un robo de barcos y un crimen de soles y de lunas.
> Duérmete. Ciérralos.
> Vi que el mar verdadero era un muchacho que saltaba desnudo,
> invitándome a un plato de estrellas y a un reposo de algas.
> ¡Sí, sí! Ya mi vida iba a ser, ya lo era, litoral desprendido.
> Pero tú, despertando, me hundiste en tus ojos.(280)

The poet's happiness, however, is shortlived, and he is suddenly submerged into an abysmal depression. Although he never specifies exactly what came between them, he implies on a number of occasions that she betrayed him: «alguien me enyesó el pecho y la sombra, / traicionándome»(281). It is interesting to note that the negative connotation of the color white is revived in this verse. In the poem «El ángel de las bodegas» a similar image is used in describing the fateful day in which he fell in love with her: «Aquel día bajé a tientas a tu alma encalada y húmeda»(281).

On a number of occasions Alberti implies that he was destined from birth to suffer this fate. In «Muerte y juicio» he recalls his childhood and refers to the blackness and uncertainty of his future as a «piedra nocturna»:

> Tizo electrocutado, infancia mía de ceniza, a mis pies, tizo yacente.
> Carbunclo hueco, negro, desprendido de un ángel que iba para piedra nocturna
> para límite entre la muerte y la nada.
> Tú: yo: niño.(282)

Alberti uses contrasting images of fire and ice to convey a similar idea in yet another verse from the same poem. The innocent child, described through various references to the color white, lies in his crib unsuspecting of the horrible fate which already has him in its grip:

> Una cuna de llamas, de norte a sur,
> de frialdad de tiza amortajada en los yelos
> a fiebre de paloma agonizando en el área de una bujía,
> una cuna de llamas, meciéndote las sonrisas, los llantos.
> Niño.(282-83)

Eric Proll believes that the nature of Alberti's poetry is not entirely personal. It is obvious, says Proll, from the number of dual references throughout the work, that Alberti is, in fact, making an analogy between his own situation and the situation of mankind in general.[22] As already seen to a certain extent in the second «Huésped de las nieblas,» a number of Alberti's images appear to have a more universal application. There are a number of verses which would appear to support Proll's argument. The verses describing the happier moments in the poet's life prior to his emotional crisis can be taken as references to an epoch when the universe was dominated by the primal elements:

> No habían cumplido años ni la rosa ni el arcángel.
> Todo, anterior al balido y al llanto.
> Cuando la luz ignoraba todavía
> si el mar nacería niño o niña.
> Cuando el viento soñaba melenas que peinar
> y claveles el fuego que encender y mejillas
> y el agua unos labios parados donde beber.
> Todo, anterior al cuerpo, al nombre y al tiempo.(278)

Following the same vein, those verses in which Alberti refers to a war

---

[22] ERIC PROLL, «The Surrealist Element in Rafael Alberti,» *Bulletin of Spanish Studies*, 14 (1941), p. 79.

which is raging within himself can be construed as references to war in general. The poem «Castigo,» for example, is full of images of war:

> Es cuando golfos y bahías de sangre,
> coagulados de astros difuntos y vengativos,
> inundan los sueños...
> Cuando saben a azufre los vientos
> y las bocas nocturnas a hueso, vidrio y alambre.(287)

While the poems are not directly social or political, some of the poet's social and political views are clearly revealed. Alberti suggests, for instance, that the ultimate downfall of mankind will come from over industrialization. «Los ángeles de las ruinas» convey that:

> La luna era muy tierna antes de los atropellos
> y solía descender a los hornos por las chimeneas de las fábricas.
> Ahora fallece impura en un mapa imprevisto de petróleo,
> asistida por un ángel que le acelera la agonía.
> Hombres de cinc, alquitrán y plomo la olvidan.(290)

A line from the same poem describes a landscape marred by railroad crossings:

> Se olvidan hombres de brea y fango
> que sus buques y sus trenes,
> a vista de pájaro,
> son ya en medio del mundo una mancha de aceite,
> limitada de cruces por todas partes.(290)

The fate of mankind, suggests the poet, like his own, is tragic, and any signs along the way are only deceiving. «Castigo» reflects this idea through contrasting images of light and dark:

> Yo no sabía que las puertas cambian de sitio,
> que las almas podían ruborizarse de sus cuerpos,
> ni que al final de un túnel la luz traía la muerte.(287)

A similar idea is expressed in «El ángel falso» through further allusions to black and white. In the poem Alberti describes life as a bad dream from which there is no awakening. The poet's hopelessness and frustration is established from the outset and reinforced by the introduction of elements which carry very definite negative connotations. Once again objects such as scissors and nails are used in this capacity. The colors are also seen in a negative light; white, in certain words which express coldness («escarcha,» «helar»), and black in the image «el luto de los cuervos»:

> ¿Para qué seguir andando?
> Las humedades son íntimas de los vidrios en punta
> y después de un mal sueño la escarcha despierta clavos
> o tijeras capaces de helar el luto de los cuervos.(289)

The conclusion of Sobre los ángeles is in part pessimistic because, «nadie espera ya la llegada del expreso, / la visita oficial de la luz a los mares necesitados»(290). His experiences, nonetheless, have brought him to one positive realization: his suffering is proof at least that he is alive:

> Pero yo os digo:
> una rosa es más rosa habitada por las orugas
> que sobre la nieve marchita de esta luna de quince años.(292)

At the end there is still one angel who survives the battle: «Todos los ángeles perdieron la vida. / Menos uno, herido, alicortado»(292). It appears, after all, that Alberti is leaving a door open, and not giving up entirely on life.

As we have attempted to show, (in this third section) Alberti sees his own tragic situation as analogous to the situation of mankind in general. There are strong indications that the poet's emotional crisis stems from an ill-fated love affair. The colors black and white are used symbolically in describing the various stages of the poet's relationship. Many of the color references, appear to contradict Alberti's normal use of them. The elements snow and ice, for example, have a different connotation than they usually have in Alberti's poetry. We can assume, therefore, that while the suggestive power of these colors is important to the poet, here they are used for their dramatic visual appeal as well.

Sobre los ángeles all too often has been referred to as Rafael Alberti's attempt at surrealism. While it is true that many of his images are surrealistic, to dismiss this work as an attempt at surrealism would be highly unjust. The work is, actually, quite realistic. It is a subjective presentation of a very real personal crisis which is taking place within the poet's own subconscious. The crisis itself is described through a series of contrasting elements of which the struggle between light and dark is the most visually apparent. The interplay of light and dark very often adds to the dramatic effect of the work. While color is one of the most important elements in Alberti's poetry, it very often serves a purely cosmetic purpose. *Sobre los ángeles,* a work practically devoid of color, is proof that the stark realities of life are often better revealed in terms of black and white.

The increasingly subjective nature of Alberti's poetry is defined by a considerable decline in the poet's use of color for merely descriptive purposes. This tendency reaches its culmination in *Sobre los ángeles,* in which the only two colors employed by the poet, black and white, are used in a highly symbolic capacity. This work is perhaps even more significant in that it marks a definite break in Alberti's color scheme. Up to now we have been able to trace the development of very distinct color patterns. In Alberti's subsequent works, which include his Civil War and post Civil War poetry, however, no obvious color patterns are revealed. Instead, the poet, for the most part, reverts back to color images he used in his earlier works in order to evoke similar moods. There are, nevertheless, some very interesting color developments as well as the poet's conception of new and interesting images which deserve consideration, and which we will be treating in the following chapters.

CHAPTER III

La sombra de los toros

The drama and pageantry of the bullfight have for centuries captured the imagination of writers and artists alike. In the 19th Century the bullfight is realistically portrayed in a series of sketches by Goya, and provides part of the scenario for Fernán Caballero's *La Gaviota*. By the turn of the century we find it harshly dealt with in Blasco Ibáñez's *Sangre y arena*. More recently, the bullfight has been a constant motif in Picasso's work and has inspired a number of the poets of the so-called «Grupo de 1927,» as evidenced by such works as Gerardo Diego's *La suerte y la muerte*, García Lorca's *Llanto por Ignacio Sánchez Mejías* and Rafael Alberti's *Verte y no verte*. While this theme reaches a new level of popularity among his contemporaries, it plays an even more significant role in the poetry of Alberti. This is, of course, understandable considering Alberti's preference for popular themes and his acute color sense.

In this chapter we will see how, through his skillfull implementation of color and imagery, Alberti successfully captures the spirit of the «corrida.» The actual spectacle of the bullfight, however, comprises only a part of Alberti's «poesía taurina.» Of far greater significance is the character of the bull itself and the psychology surrounding the animal. The bull takes on two contradictory symbolic connotations in Alberti's poetry. On the one hand, it is a symbol of death and destruction that inspires the poet's fear and his wrath. On the other hand, it is a pathetic figure which arouses the poet's love and compassion.

Marinero en tierra offers the first series of images associated with the figure of the bull. «¡Jee, compañero, jee, jee! / ¡Un toro azul por el agua!»[1] But it is not until *El alba del alhelí* that the theme of bullfighting is given any real consideration. In the first part of our chapter we will examine three poems from this work in which Alberti's interest in this theme is reflected: «El Niño de la Palma,» «Joselito en su gloria» and «Seguidillas a una extranjera.» Each composition depicts one particular aspect of the bullfight: the playfullness of the «torero» in the face of death, the tragedy of the «cogida,» and the anguish of a beautiful woman spectator. Next we will look at «Corrida de toros» and «Palco» from Alberti's subsequent work *Cal y Canto*. These two classic examples of Gongoran verse are replete with colorful images and poetic visions. Our next area of interest is Alberti's Civil War poetry, more specifically, the section «Toro en el mar» from his book *Entre el clavel y la espada* where

---

[1] RAFAEL ALBERTI, *Poesías completas* (Buenos Aires: Losanda, 1961), p. 72.

Spain is symbolized as a wounded and agonizing bull. For the first time Alberti's images appear to have an emotional appeal as well as a visual appeal: «El toro en la poesía de Alberti se individualiza, es en ella más que un emblema o un signo, es él quien carga con la herida y a veces con la angustia.»[2] The image of Spain in the form of a wounded bull is continued in «Egloga fúnebre» from the book *Pleamar*. The poem is a dialogue among four voices, three of which are the voices of Antonio Machado, García Lorca and Miguel Hernández. The fourth voice is that of the bull. The conversation concerns the fate of the animal. Images of death contrast sharply with other images which recall what life was like before the war brought chaos and destruction to Spain. Lastly we will examine Alberti's now famous elegy on the death of the bullfighter Ignacio Sánchez Mejías, *Verte y no verte,* in which the bull is seen in a totally different light. While in García Lorca's poem *Llanto por la muerte de Ignacio Sánchez Mejías* the poet's attention is focused on the bullfighter, in Alberti's poem primary consideration is given to the bull itself, whose haunting presence is felt throughout the poem, from his very conception to his death.

Corridas de toros

Through his use of dynamic and colorful images, Alberti succeeds in *El alba del alhelí* in taking the reader beyond the realm of reality and projects him into what Eric Proll refers to as «an atmosphere of semi-impressionism.»[3] In the poem «El Niño de la Palma,» several very notable characteristics of the bullfighter are depicted: his uncanny sense of elusiveness and physical agility, the reckless abandon with which he approaches his confrontation with the bull, and his defiant attitude toward death. Alberti explains that this pose is typical of the bullfighter: «Este arriesgar el cuerpo bailando, esta fiesta española de ganar y perder, yo la he visto encarnada en el toreo.»[4] The bullfighter in «El Niño de la Palma» is very typical in this respect. His defiance of death recalls, as Solita Salinas de Marichal points out, a similar defiant attitude in Lope's *Caballero de Olmedo*:[5]

¡Qué salero!
¡Cógeme, torillo fiero!
Te dije y te lo repito
para no comprometerte,
que tenga cuernos la muerte
a mí se me importa un pito.(179)

---

[2] LUIS DE CARVAJAL, «Presencia y ausencia de la nostalgia,» *Tres L,* 8 (1941), p. 110.

[3] ERIC PROLL, «Popularismo and Barroquismo in the Poetry of Rafael Alberti,» *Bulletin of Spanish Studies,* 14 (1942), p. 70.

[4] SOLITA SALINAS DE MARICHAS, *El mundo poético de Rafael Alberti* (Madrid: Gredos, 1968), p. 140. [Solita Salinas de Marichal does not indicate the source of this quotation.]

[5] Ibid., p. 143.

The elusiveness of the bullfighter is seen through a series of air related images which suggest quickness and agility. In one verse he is described in birdlike terms:

> ¡Aire, que al toro torillo
> le pica el pájaro pillo
> que no pone el pie en el suelo! (178)

A similar image is employed in a subsequent verse in which the bullfighter is said to have wings on his slippers and on his pauldrons:

> Alas en las zapatillas,
> céfiros en las hombreras,...(179)

Alberti's use of the color yellow is significant in the construction of images of this nature. Yellow or gold signifies two things. It is the color of the bullfighter's costume, the traditional «traje de luces.» It is also associated with light and movement, and is used to reinforce those images which express these qualities. In one verse, for example, the bullfighter is described as a «gorrión de oro»(179). Other times the color is evoked through a more suggestive image, as in the example, «canario de las barreras»(179).
«Joselito en su gloria» evokes an entirely different mood. The horror of death which is expressed in the poem contrasts sharply with the playful tone of «El Niño de la Palma.» The concentration of color reflects the change in mood. Joselito is described as, «Niño de amaranto y oro,...»(175). Gold again refers to the color of his «traje de luces,» while «amaranto» expresses the color of the blood which now stains it. Other references to the color red include this typically Gongoran image of the mortally wounded bullfighter, in which the blood spewing forth from the bullfighter's wound is likened to bubbling rubies, and the bloodstains to red roses:

> Mírame así, chorreado
> de un borbotón de rubíes
> que ciñe de carmesíes
> rosas mi talle quebrado.(176)

In another verse the poet borrows an image from a «canción popular» in describing the bullfighter's severe loss of blood:

> Virgen de la Macarena,
> mírame tú cómo vengo,
> tan sin sangre, que ya tengo
> blanca mi color morena.(176)

The third poem in this series, «Seguidillas a una extranjera,» is a description of a woman spectator vicariously experiencing the horror of the bullfight:

> Y tú, arriba, en los palcos

77

crucificada
desgarrándote el pecho
con una espada.(177-178)

The woman's anguish is conveyed through an elaborate pattern of images in which she is compared to several flowers. In one verse she is described as «arrebolera,» a reference to her rosy complexion. She is also called «pasionaria,» although it is not so much the color of the flower (purple and white) the poet is alluding to here, but the fact that the flower itself is generally associated with the Passion of Christ and is, consequently, a symbol of the woman's suffering. The suggestive capacity of color is best reflected perhaps in the following image in which the color red or purple, evoked by the word «mora,» refers to both the spilled blood in the arena, as well as to the woman's sense of horror upon seeing it:

Gracia negra, de fuego,
tras los percales,
pintándolos de moras
de los morales.(177)

Dos poemas gongorinos

In *Cal y canto* bullfighting continues to be a source of inspiration for the poet. Two poems of particular interest are «Corrida de toros» and «Palco.» In many respects these two poems resemble those cited from *El alba del alhelí*. But now the poet's images are more suggestive and include a much wider range of colors. In «Corrida de toros» the conflict between man and beast is captured through a series of very complex poetic visions. The first verse of the poem sets the stage for the conflict:

De sombra, sol y muerte, volandera
grana zumbando, el ruedo gira herido
por un clarín de sangre azul torera.(208)

Each of the three nouns in the first verse, «sombra,» «sol» and «muerte,» is significant in the construction of the poem. The words «sol» and «sombra» refer, of course, to the sun and shade of the bullring. The word «sombra,» however, refers also to the bull. The word implies all of the characteristics of the beast: his color, his size, as well as his ominous presence in the bullring. The word «sol,» likewise, refers to the bullfighter. Whereas the bull is usually described in terms of darkness, the bullfighter is almost always described in terms of light. The word «muerte» refers to the imminent outcome of the drama. The images «volandera grana zumbando» and «herido por un clarín de sangre azul torera» can be interpreted in two ways. On the one hand the poet is describing the bullring itself, which appears to come to life with the trumpet call announcing the start of the day's events. «Volandera grana zumbando» is also an allusion to the wounded bull, while «un clarín de sangre azul torera,» an excellent example of synaesthesia, refers to the sword thrust which leaves him mortally wounded. Although neither the word «clarín» nor the expression «sangre azul» visually reminds the reader of a sword, there are qualities inherent in each which evoke a similar emotional response. The more traditional association of «sangre azul» with nobility does not appear to be implied here. The color blue suggests instead coldness, a characteristic of the sword, while the word «clarín» brings to mind a piercing sound. The key to this image, however, is the word «herido» which allows us to draw the association between these two images.

As the conflict develops, the interplay between light and dark becomes more and more apparent. In one verse, for example, the bull is compared to a dark stormy sea and the bullfighter to a lighthouse:

> Se hace añicos el aire, y violento,
> un mar, por media luna mandado,
> prende fuego a un farol que apaga el viento.(209)

The expression, «por media luna mandado,» an image Alberti borrowed from Lope and which is used repeatedly in his «poesía taurina,» is a reference to the horns of the bull.

Continuing the imagery along these same lines, Alberti compares in a subsequent verse the bull's back to the waves of the sea. The «banderillas» which transform the bull's back into a «verbena de sangre» are likened to the masts of ships bobbing up and down in a sea of blood:

> Cinco picas al monte, y cinco olas
> sus lomos empinados convirtiendo
> en verbena de sangre y banderolas.(209)

The interplay of light and shadow is also apparent in the following verse in which the poet makes reference to the various gestures and poses of the «torero»:

> Brindis, cristiana mora, a ti, volando,
> cuervo mudo y sin ojos, la montera
> del áurea espada, que en el sol lidiando
> y en la sombra, vendido, de puntillas,
> da su junco a la media luna fiera,
> y a la muerte su gracia, de rodillas.(209)

The more obvious antithetical elements are the references to «sol y sombra» and to the two poses of the bullfighter: «de puntillas,» the pose the bullfighter assumes during the actual moment of truth, and «de rodillas,» the humble gesture of kneeling before the crowd. The poet alludes also to the noble gesture of tossing the cap, «cuervo mudo y sin ojos,» to a woman in the crowd as a token of esteem, and to the ceremonious raising of the sword, «áurea espada,» for all to see.

Another excellent example of the descriptive capacity of color in the poem is the reference to the bullfighter as, «Veloz, rayo de plata en campo de oro, / nacido de la arena y suspendido / por un estambre, de la gloria, al toro...»(209). The poetic technique of synecdoche is skillfully employed by the poet in this image. The bullfighter is painted in both silver, the color of his sword, and gold, the color of the sand of the bullring. Thus, the bullfighter, the bull, and the bullring itself are all fused into one harmonious body.

The young woman spectator introduced earlier in «Seguidillas a una extranjera,» reappears in the poems of *Cal y canto.* As in Alberti's earlier poem, the flower imagery is quite apparent. In «Corrida de toros» she is described as «rosa en el palco de la muerte aún viva, / libre y por fuera sanguinaria y dura, / pero de corza el corazón, cautiva»(209). Like the rose she is fragile although outwardly she appears to be unaffected by the events. In «Palco» she is once again likened to a flower. The poet emphasizes above all the woman's anguish by referring to her as «asesinada flor de los balcones»(209). In this poem, however, the flower imagery comprises only a small part of a much more complex network of images which attempt to draw a parallel between the suffering of the animal and her own suffering. A number of the poet's images are designed specifically to be interpreted both as references to the woman as well as to the bull. The most easily recognizable point of comparison is the visual similarity between the two based on the color black. The bull, as we have previously noted, is usually described in Alberti's poetry in terms of darkness. In the first verse of «Palco» the woman is referred to as «Gacela sin fanal» and «cruz sin faroles»(210). In a subsequent verse the poet alludes to the color in a specific reference to the woman's attire: «... virgen sola, / que arrastrabas la noche en los vestidos»(210). The association between the woman and the bull is made even more convincing through a dual symbolic reference. The suffering of the bull, which parallels her own suffering, is symbolized in the figure of La Dolorosa, a Madonna whose heart is pierced by seven swords:

Gacela sin faroles, sepultado
por siete bayonetas, no de flores,
el corazón sin pulso y resultado,...

Siete toros, amor, y siete espadas,
rayos rectos en curva, los tendidos
remontando y fijándose, clavadas

En ti, centro del mundo...(210)

The final outcome of the conflict ultimately depends on her actions. By a mere waving of her handkerchief, the bull is condemned to death:

Sigues muerta, imperante desde el cielo
y pendiente el escándalo del toro
de los picos sin sol de tu pañuelo.(211)

The phrase «los picos sin sol» is one of the many omens of death which appear in this and other poems relating to the bullfight; omens which indicate that the fate of the bull is pre-determined. By condemning the bull to death, she is, in a sense condemning herself to a symbolic death. To round out and complete the analogy, the poet reverts to the flower imagery with which he began the poem, but now he applies it to the bull as well. In his defeated state the bull is compared to a flower which, though once in bloom, has since lost its color and withered:

> flor de percal, que, abierta en los corrales,
> entre siete relámpagos de oro
> moriste en las barandas celestiales.(211)

Hence, through a series of images which evoke light and darkness, Alberti is able to capture the mood of the conflict between man and beast. Later, in his Civil War poetry, the images of darkness begin to outweigh the images of light. The atmosphere of the bullring is replaced by an atmosphere of war and destruction in which the figure of the bull assumes even greater significance.

Toro en el mar

The Spanish Civil War was a major crisis in Alberti's life. The war affected Alberti very deeply. He saw cities razed, close friends murdered, and dreams he had sought vanish. He was eventually forced to abandon his country, and has since been living in exile. Feelings of bitterness and deprivation pervade all of Alberti's post-Civil War poetry.

Alberti's first post-Civil War work, whose main theme concerns the war, is *Entre el clavel y la espada*. One of the more compelling sections of the book is «Toro en el mar,» subtitled «Elegía sobre un mapa perdido.» In the poems of this section, the central image is Spain symbolically presented as a wounded and agonizing bull. A number of earth images are associated with the animal.

Prior to this work, the element «earth» or «tierra» had unfavorable connotations in Alberti's poetry. In *Marinero en tierra*, for example, Alberti often implies that he feels insecure on land: «Me perdí en la tierra»(60). In *Sobre los ángeles* «la tierra» is said to be inhabited by shadows and is described as a barren region where there is no life:

> Y el mar fue y le dio un nombre,
> y un apellido el viento.
> y las nubes un cuerpo
> y un alma el fuego.
> La tierra, nada.

> Ese reino movible,
> colgado de las águilas,
> no la conoce.

> Nunca escribió su sombra
> la figura de un hombre.(267)

In another verse from this same work, the earth is the domain of fools:
«¡El ángel tonto! / ¡Si será de la tierra! / —Sí, de la tierra sólo»(272).
In Alberti's post-Civil War poetry, however, the element «tierra» has a
very different connotation. It is an object of love, the traditional mother-
image which evokes the poet's love and respect. The bull, which was
previously a symbol of force and destruction in Alberti's poetry, suffers
a similar transformation. In «Toro en el mar» he is a beast to be loved
and pitied, a beast that epitomizes the pain and anguish of a war-torn
country.

The basic image Alberti employs is visual. He compares Spain to the
hide of a bull stretched out over the sea:

> Tienes forma de toro,
> de piel de toro abierto,
> tendido sobre el mar.(471)

Alberti's image is similar to León Felipe's, «España... ¡es el hacha!».
Each of these images, the hatchet blade and the hide of the bull stretched
out, physically resembles the shape of the country. The similarity between
Alberti's image and Felipe's image is not just visual. Both images suggest
violence. Alberti's image, however, offers a greater range of symbolic
possibilities. The term «piel de toro,» for example, suggests a mere remnant
of the animal it once was. The sea upon which the hide of the bull is
stretched is described as a sea of blood:

> Mira, en aquel país
> ahora se puede navegar en sangre.(471)

Through his use of vivid colors, Alberti is able to dramatize the
changes brought about by the war. Some of the poems recall what life
was like before the conflict brought death and destruction:

> Eras jardín de naranjas,
> huerta de mares abiertos.
> Tiemblo de olivas y de pámpanos,
> los verdes cuernos.(471)

In each of these connotations, the bull is described in terms which
correspond to the land: «jardín de naranjas,» «huerta,» «tiemblo de olivas
y de pámpanos». The color green, which is directly mentioned only once
but implied in a number of the images, is an obvious symbol of life.

Occasionally these images of life, again reinforced by the poet's use
of the color green, are juxtaposed with images of fire and destruction
which are, in turn, reinforced by the use of the colors, red and black:

> ¡Ay verde toro, ay,

THE POETRY OF RAFAEL ALBERTI

que eras toro de trigo,
toro de lluvia y sol, de cierzo y nieve,
triste hoguera atizada hoy en medio del mar,
del mar, del mar ardiendo.(474-75)

Almost all of Alberti's descriptions of war utilize red and black. The fields appear to have been fertilized with gunpowder: «Con pólvora te regaron. / Y fuiste toro de fuego»(471). Another verse describes how the bull has been nurtured on black bile and brave soldier's blood:

Le están dando a ese toro
pastos amargos,
yerbas con sustancia de muertos,
negras hieles
y clara sangre ingenua de soldado.(472)

Alberti's use of the colors black and red is especially effective in the following verse in which the elements of nature seem to share in the bull's suffering: «Todo oscuro, terrible. Aquella luna / que se rompió, de pronto, echando sangre»(495).

The mood changes as the poet describes the aftermath of the war. The bull would like to believe that the war was just a bad dream from which he will soon awake:

Querías despertarte, pobre toro,
abrumada de nieblas la cabeza.
Querías sacudir la hincada cola
y el obligado párpado caído refrescarlo en el mar,
mojándote de verde las pupilas.
Resollabas de sangre, rebasado, abarcado,
oprimido de noche y de terrores,
bramando por abrir una brecha en el cielo
y sonrosarte un poco de dulce aurora
los despoblados ramos de tus astas.(478)

The green of the sea and the white of the dawn can be interpreted as signs of a possible rebirth. As is often the case, the color green is accompanied here by references to the element water, another symbol of life.

The poet also has a vision. He imagines that the bull has died but that his soul has risen. The terrestrial bull has become a celestial bull reminiscent somewhat of Góngora's «Mentido robador de Europa»: «Todos creíamos. / La noche se ha vuelto toro»(481). In his vision the poet conceives of himself as a god capable of recreating night and day, which are figuratively represented in the poem as pastures of silver and gold upon which the celestial bull can graze. He comes to realize, however, that there is in fact no celestial bull, only a mere «sombra»:

Abrí la puerta.
En donde no había camino,

vi una vereda.
Anduve.

Anduve, y a los dos lados,
bien dormido, iba sembrando:
al uno, pasto de plata;
al otro, dorado.

Cuando volvía,
como una sombra, vi un toro,
llorando.(482)

These verses offer some insight into Alberti's own feelings about Spain.
The poet, although he has chosen to live in exile as a result of the outcome
of the war, hopes of someday returning to his homeland and playing an
instrumental role in its future rebuilding. He realizes that this too is
merely a dream which may never be fulfilled.

Alberti, nevertheless, ends this section on an optimistic note. Though
far from his native land, he can still hear signs of life coming from its
shores: «Pobre toro lejano, / te oigo bramar»(483). The bull is not dead
after all and will someday recover the grandeur it had once known:

Cornearás aún y más que nunca,
desdoblando los campos de tu frente,
y salpicando valles y laderas
te elevarás de nuevo toro verde.(483)

Egloga fúnebre

The pathetic image of Spain as the hide of a bull floating in a sea
of blood is presented again, perhaps even more forcefully, in Alberti's
«Egloga fúnebre» from the collection of poems entitled *Pleamar*. «Egloga
fúnebre» is a rather long poem in the form of a drama. The characters
of the drama include a narrator, three voices, which represent the poets
Antonio Machado, García Lorca and Miguel Hernández, all victims of the
war, and one bull, who, as in «Toro en el mar,» symbolizes Spain. The
setting is a barren and desolate land which has been ravaged by war:
«La tierra que divide no es ya tierra, / que es taladro, garganta solamente / para tragar la muerte de la vida»(541). All life-giving elements have
become stagnated. There is no movement in the sea or the air: «Fijo
en sus ondas, que no van al mar, / fijo en su brisa, que ni va ni viene»(541).

As in «Toro en el mar,» images of death and destruction are in contrast
with images of life which recall what Spain was before the war:

Un toro derribado,
junto a la orilla,
herido.
Su piel son agujeros

de sangre rota y penas,
por los que asoma y brilla
entumecido
un pasado de azules ganaderos,
hoy de lirios violetas y azucenas.(543)

The poet's past is described in terms of the color blue, which although not usually used in this capacity is, in this verse, symbolic of life. The present is described by images of mourning: «lirios violetas y azucenas.» More common, however, are references to the past in terms of the color green:

Cuando mi clara voz se hizo neblina
y se me fue pasando
de rama verde de olivar a encina.(543)

Al hombre de la esteva y la guadaña
lo empiné a eternas, verdes maravillas
de onduladas alturas candeales,(543)

The color green is indirectly alluded to in the latter verse in the words «esteva» y «guadaña,» tools used in harvesting crops. Once again the color is accompanied by other symbols of life, water and air, which are evoked by the image «onduladas alturas candeales.»

The war itself is depicted in terms of a bullfight, but, unlike some of Alberti's poems of this nature in which the bull represents all that is negative, here the animal is the object of the poet's sympathies:

¡A ese toro!   Le entierren entre cardos la lengua,
después que lo lancinen hasta en los ojos picas,
banderillas de pólvora le empujen en los huesos
y una espada candente le hinque el testuz...(545)

The violence and horror of the bullfight are dramatized in the poet's effective use of the color red. In the following verse, for example, a comparison is drawn between a foreboding moon and the wounded bull: «la luna, atado el cuello, rebotando, / roja, de peña en peña, descornada»(549). Alberti describes the moon by employing a simple visual image, yet the words he choses («atado el cuello» and «descornada») are terms which are more appropriate in describing the bull. Even when the color red is not mentioned directly, it is strongly suggested in the poet's choice of words, especially in the repetition of «sangre»:

Gire ese toro, gire, abierto, desollado,
fijo sobre un mar de sangre navegable.(545)

Y hasta las vidas ya eran fuentes de sangre.(547)

85

The final scene where the dead bull is dragged out of the arena, is a very colorful vision:

> La tarde va de huida por escaleras granas,
> y por la mar un toro, desvanecido, a rastras,
> bajo un redoble mustio de espumas y retamas.(550)

Here the personified afternoon fleeing down a red stairway seems to accompany the dead bull, in its journey over the sea to the drumbeat of the waves upon the shore.

Like «Toro en el mar,» «Egloga fúnebre» also ends on an optimistic note. Amidst all of these visions of death and destruction, there remains some hope. The bull, though mortally wounded, makes one final attempt to embrace life:

> (Aquí el toro gritó, crujió tan fieramente,
> como si con garganta de monte; si con lengua
> de borrasca o con pozos de truenos se pudiera.
> Tan herido y tan duro, que hasta en el río exánime
> tembló helado papel la cara de la muerte,
> subiendo a torrenciales auroras los olivos
> y a festones de luz el mar enguirnaldado.
> Fue como si de pronto un boreal augurio,
> una alegre catástrofe sin fin se derramara
> bajo los delirantes abrazos de los puentes.) (552)

What a symphonic «despedida»! Nature and many of its components appear to bid adieu to the extinct animal which once «había pisado» that land and perhaps dreamed in unison with the variegated light of the day.

Verte y no verte

Rafael Alberti's «poesía taurina» is best exemplified by his now famous elegy on the death of Ignacio Sánchez Mejías, *Verte y no verte*. Alberti's poem has been somewhat overshadowed by Lorca's *Llanto por Ignacio Sánchez Mejías*. The two works, however, are quite different. Lorca's poem is written as though the poet were physically present and witnessing the tragic event. The reader's attention remains focused on the event by the repetition of such haunting lines as, «a las cinco de la tarde» and « ¡Que no quiero verla! » Alberti's poem, on the other hand emphasizes the distance between the poet and the event: «Verte y no verte. / Yo, lejos navegando; / tú, por la muerte»(359). Lorca's poem also stresses primarily the bullfighter's death and the effect it has on him while Alberti's composition emphasizes more the psychology behind the tragedy.

Verte y no verte is structurally divided into four sections each bearing the same heading, «El toro de la muerte,» and an epilogue entitled «Dos arenas.» Each section, subdivided into three parts, begins with a rigidly constructed sonnet in which the bull is described. Alberti does not refer specifically to the bull that killed Ignacio Sánchez Mejías but rather to the incarnation of a concept: a bull which represents force, passion, and an unrelenting, almost masochistic desire for conflict and death. The sonnet is followed by verses in italics which convey the poet's own thoughts. These verses are in the form of the traditional «seguidilla.» The third part of each section consists primarily of a loosely constructed subjective stanza accompanied at the end by seven lines in italics. Herein are reflected the bullfighter's own subconscious thoughts. The epilogue, «Dos arenas,» also written in the form of a sonnet, ties together the present and the past in an attempt to show that although the bullfighter has died, his spirit lives on.

The bright vivid colors which are generally associated with the bullfight are absent in this poem. As Juan José Cuadros points out, «el color...se borra en una aguada oscura, quedando en las manchas, sólo el blanco de los quirófanos, lo rojo de la sangre, el negro de la suerte.»[6] Although red, black and white are the only colors Alberti employs, he applies them skillfully. The colors emerge through an intricate web of images which depict the bullfight as a continual struggle between a number of antithetical elements. The most common of these elements are darkness and light. In one verse the bullfight is described as, «sombra armada contra luz armada»(359). The «torero» is described by both images of light and related images of air which, like light, is generally a symbol of life. There are references to the bullfighter as a «mariposa de rojo y amarillo»(360), «golondrina»(360), «gaviota»(360) and «paloma»(360). The bull likewise is described by images of darkness and related images of land, both of which are symbols of death in Alberti's poetry.

The first «toro de la muerte» is the unborn bull still in its mother's womb:

> En el oscuro germen desceñido
> que dentro de la vaca proporciona
> los pulsos a la sangre que sazona
> la fiereza del toro no nacido;
> antes de tu existir, antes de nada,
> se enhebraron un duro pensamiento
> las no floridas puntas de tu frente.(359)

The reference to the fetus as an «oscuro germen» has an almost ominous ring to it, while the simple mention of the word «sangre» implies passion and fury.

The second «toro de la muerte» is the bull grazing in the pasture and anxiously awaiting his encounter with the bullfighter:

> Negro toro, nostálgico de heridas,
> corneándole al agua sus paisajes,
> ... ...
> Nostálgico de un hombre con la espada,
> de sangre femoral y de gangrena
> ni el mayoral ya puede detenerte.(360)

---

[6] Juan José Cuadros, «En torno a una elegía, *Verte y no verte*, de Rafael Alberti,» *Cuadernos Hispanoamericanos*, 68 (1966), p. 188.

As in the first «toro de la muerte,» the emphasis is on the ultimate destiny of the animal. The color black is again used in reference to the bull. He is called «Negro toro.» Red is strongly suggested in the expression «de sangre femoral y de gangrena.» The bullfighter himself has a premonition of death: «Así, con medias rosas y zapatillas negras me va a matar la muerte»(361), and, in his desire to free himself from his tragic fate, he calls out for air, a symbol of life: «¡Aire! »(360).

The third «toro de la muerte» is the bull finally prepared to meet the object of his destiny. Using images of fire in order to emphasize the violent passion with which he awaits the encounter, Alberti exclaims: «toro tizón, humo y candela, / que ardiendo de los cuernos a la cola, / de la noche saldrás carbonizado»(362). The bull is also compared to a lava flow: «tuérzale el cuello al rumbo de esa roja avalancha de toros»(365). In contrast to these fire images a number of water images are introduced. In one verse the poet attempts to dissuade the bull by asking him to cool his passions by directing his energies toward the sea: «Corre, toro, a la mar, embiste, nada, / y a un torero de espuma, sal y arena, / ya que intentas herir, dale la muerte»(361). In another verse that serves to emphasize the tragic outcome, the bullfighter tells the bull that his efforts will not provide him water as in the pastures, but blood:

> Me buscas como a un montón de arena donde escarbar un hoyo,
> sabiendo que en el fondo no vas a encontrar agua,
> no vas a encontrar agua,
> nunca jamás tú vas a encontrar agua,
> sino sangre,
> no agua,
> jamás
> nunca.(364)

But the «torero's» plea for life, symbolized by water, goes unheeded:

> déjame toda el agua,
> le pido que me deje para mí solo toda el agua,
> agua libre,
> río libre.(365)

The fourth «toro de la muerte» deals with the clash between beast and man, in which the latter is left mortally wounded: «Al fin diste a tu duro pensamiento / forma mortal de lumbre derribada»(364). Again the bullfighter is «lumbre derribada,» a fate that later was to befall the bull also when he becomes «sombra en derribo»(365).

The actual «cogida» is presented with «Mas clavaste por fin bajo el estribo, / con puntas de rencor tintas en ira, / tu oscuridad, hasta empalidecerte»(365). The conflict between light and darkness is again suggested in the words «oscuridad» and «empalidecerte.» The horns of the bull are seen as «puntas de rencor tintas en ira.» Alberti chooses the word «ira» rather than «sangre» because it more strongly conveys the feeling without destroying the image.

Thus, the tragic death of Ignacio Sánchez Mejías is depicted as a psychological struggle between the forces of life and death through Alberti's effective use of three colors and a complex network of antithetical images. «La corrida de toros» is a part of Spain's culture that is very much ingrained in its people. Through his poetry, Rafael Alberti shows that he has not lost touch with the popular element as did so many of the poets of his generation. The color, excitement, and tragedy of the bullfight are visually real and Alberti seems to have captured its drama with his unique color schemes.

CHAPTER IV

El color de la memoria

Rafael Alberti was one of the more politically active members of the «Generación del 27.» During the years 1934-1936, just prior to the outbreak of the Spanish Civil War, Alberti traveled extensively throughout Russia, France, the United States, México and Cuba. He presented lectures and sought support for the cause of the Asturian revolutionaries. He returned to Spain in 1936 in the midst of the turmoil and actively participated in a number of anti-fascist organizations including the «Alianza de Intelectuales Antifascistas» of which he was later named secretary. Alberti remained in Spain throughout the greater part of the war; but when the tide began to turn in favor of the fascists, he regretfully abandoned his homeland and went to Paris. Shortly after his arrival there, the Second World War began and, faced with the prospect of living through yet another war, he chose to leave Paris. He and his wife moved to the politically neutral country, Argentina, where he continued to be haunted by the memories of war, the death of many of his close friends, and a sense of political defeat.

In terms of his poetry, Alberti's Civil War years and those immediately following are not very productive. As C. B. Morris points out, each of Alberti's attempts at developing new themes proves to be a failure. «It is a pity,» says Morris, «that a man capable of doing with words what painters achieve with a brush could not have recognized in his seemingly endless and undistinctive verses about his dog, daughter and politics a recurrent poetic exhaustion which self-discipline and discrimination could have cured.»[1] He is forced to look to the past in order to recover that seemingly lost thread of poetic inspiration. Hence, his most sincere poetic expression is found in those verses in which he nostalgically recalls experiences of his past and relates them to his existence at the time:

> Tras alegrías y sombras, tras el combate y la vigilia, la presencia del recuerdo, la atracción de lo pasado vivo en la memoria, recreado sin cesar en la imaginación, aparece como la tendencia última y más entrañable del poeta.[2]

---

[1] C. B. MORRIS, *A Generation of Spanish Poets* (Cambridge: Cambridge Univ. Press, 1969), p. 241.
[2] RICARDO GULLÓN, «Alegrías y sombras de Rafael Alberti,» *Insula*, 198 (May 1963), p. 1.

The slightest reminder of his past serves as an inspiration to him. The campfires in the fields recall the bitter memories of war. The clouds in the sky take on the shape of a map of Spain. But at the crux of Alberti's nostalgia, is the element, which, from the beginning, served as his basic source of poetic inspiration: the sea.

> Cuando se. entró la noche
> y apenas le veía,
> era su opaca voz,
> era tal vez la sombra
> de su voz la que hablaba
> todavía del mar,
> del mar como si acaso
> no fuera a llegar nunca.(823)

For Alberti, the sea is the only reality that remains unchanged, or as the poet himself says, «Sola la mar permanece»(607). In Alberti's «poesía de la posguerra» the sea acquires a special significance. It becomes a fountain of youth which metaphorically takes the poet back to his childhood.

Nostalgia is not a recent theme in Alberti's poetry, nor is it exclusive to his post-Civil War poetry. In fact, this longing can be traced back to Alberti's *Marinero en tierra* where he evoked memories of the pleasant and carefreee days of his childhood in Puerto de Santa María. On the imagined visits of this period his retinue is large. The war, the people he has known or places he has visited accompany him, but he is obliged to reveal that his allusions are also brought occasionally with bitterness and regret.

One of the more notable characteristics of Alberti's post-Civil War poetry is the appreciable decline in the poet's use of color. The horrors of war and other bitter experiences are reflected in the poet's symbolic use of such colors as red and black which are very often found in contrast to the white, green and blue of former «recuerdos,» but even these have limited application. The only works in which color is still a more or less significant element, are *Pleamar, Retornos de lo vivo lejano, Baladas y canciones del Paraná,* and *A la pintura,* which will be treated separately in Chapter VI.

Tiene el volver, color de mar

The first book Alberti writes while in exile is *Pleamar.* It is a loosely constructed collection of poems subdivided into eight rather short segments: «Aitana,» the first of these segments, is dedicated to the poet's daughter; «Arión,» «Cármenes» and «Versos sueltos para una exposición» are short stanzas with wandering references to the sea and the air; «Tirteo» concerns the horrors of war; «Egloga fúnebre,» treated separately in the previous chapter, also recalls the Spanish Civil War: «Invitación a un viaje sonoro» presents a series of poems in a musical context. Many of the poems are based on the songs and dances of a particular region; finally, there is an untitled section which includes a number of poems which pay homage to some of the world's great poets and writers.

One of the first striking impressions produced upon reading *Pleamar* is the apparent similiarity to *Marinero en tierra*. A number of the poems concern themselves with the sea. Consequently, many of the colors and images relating to the sea are the same. However, the overall mood of each of these works is noticeably different. The poems of *Pleamar* exude an overwhelming sense of vagueness and distance which contrasts sharply with the clarity with which Alberti recalled his childhood in *Marinero en tierra*. This difficulty in relating to his past is revealed in a number of ways. One of the more obvious is perhaps the elemental framework. While the sea is central call to both works, in *Pleamar* the less tangible element, air, comes into play. Air and sea are often fused and the individual qualities of one are passed on to the other creating a somewhat vague and ethereal mood: «La luz domina los espacios y trae la antigua sonrisa del mar en su ala mensajera. El mar, más claro, más maduro 'de pleno azul y antigua transparencia,' tanto que se funde con el aire.»[3] Another element which plays a significant role in conveying the poet's sense of disorientation is color. The colors most often found throughout the work are the greens, blues and whites of the «mar gaditana.» But in *Pleamar* these colors seem to have a certain transparency they did not possess earlier. Were we to draw an analogy between Alberti's poetry and painting, we would probably describe the poems of *Marinero en tierra* as oil paintings and the poems of *Pleamar* as watercolors. In the poem «Aitana,» for example, Alberti asks the sea to lend some of its beauty to his daughter. The poet gives the sea, however, only a touch of blue: «Mares más lejanas, dadle vuestra belleza; / tu breve añil...»(509). The color white is evoked by the equally diaphanous image, «el respiro blanco de la espuma»(509). «Elegía a una vida clara y hermosa» presents a landscape where «Sueñe el bosque su verde transparencia»(567). Another poem tells «Como por transparencia / se ve subir, abrir súbitamente, / más que jazmín, doblado jazminero, / pura, desvanecida, delicada»(564).

Many of the visions of *Pleamar* convey a sense of fleetingness or fugacity. The melting snow and the galloping horse are introduced in this capacity. In the poem «Vaivén,» for example, the snow becomes a symbol of the poet's frustrated desire to attain the unattainable:

> Ya nieve azul a la ida,
> nieve lila al retornar,
> yo quiero pisar la nieve
> azul del jacarandá.(571)

The colors blue and lilac applied to the snow are in themselves symbols of the unattainable and, therefore, add to the overall sense of magical

---

[3] Solita Salinas de Marichal, «Los paraísos perdidos,» *Insula*, 198 (May 1963), p. 10.

mystery. The image of the galloping horse is even more prevalent in this work, and is used primarily in reference to bodies of water or to the air. «Remontando los ríos,» transforms the rivers into: «Ríos caballos, ríos / de colas levantadas, / ríos ciegos, a tumbos, / heridos por las ramas»(512). The surf (in a poem from «Arión») becomes wild horses:

> Feroces leones.
> Furiosos caballos.
> Mas si son de espuma,
> ¿quién podrá domarlos?(525)

When the image is repeated and color added in another composition, the visual effect is more prominent: «De pronto, el mar suelta un caballo blanco... / y se queda dormido»(525). The galloping horse replaces the wind in «Hemisferio austral» where «De caballos reverdece el viento»(518). Occasionally both images, the melting snow and the galloping horse, are fused. The poem «Rusia,» for example, seeks an answer: «Es la nieve, ésa es la nieve, / ¿Es un caballo la nieve? / ¿Avanza, llega, se pierde?»(602).

The colors and images used in conveying the poet's state of mind are reinforced by the repetion of the word «desorientado» throughout the work:

> Desorientado, subo de las blandas,
> dormidas superficies
> que dan casa a mi sueño.(570)
> ... ...
> La luz, el aire, la sal.
> El ángel que al quiebro vuela,
> desorientado, a un rosal
> de alegre miel sobre hojuela.(572)
> ... ...
> Nana, que las veletas
> giran desorientadas.(513)

Thus it can be stated that the elemental framework of the book, the transparency of the colors, and the elusive nature of the images, combine to convey the poet's nostalgia, his disorientation and his difficulty in relating to his remote past.

Retorno a través de los colores

The theme of nostalgia is most lucidly presented in the work *Retornos de lo vivo lejano*. The book is divided into three sections. The first contains poems recalling the poet's childhood: his home, his family and his schooldays. The second, «Retornos del amor,» is, as the title suggests, a collection of poems about Alberti's own experiences in love. The nature of these compositions is vague, and one is not certain whether the poet is referring to a love affair with a woman or a love affair with nature.

94

The third section includes a variety of poems which relive special moments in Alberti's life or evoke memories of lost friends.

Unlike *Pleamar,* in which Alberti seems to be struggling to find some sort of identity, in *Retornos de lo vivo lejano* he appears to have found it. It becomes obvious that Alberti has formulated by this time a much clearer perspective on life. Rafael Lozana discusses the poet's newly acquired sense of self awareness and the poetic maturity revealed in this work when he states:

> Es en *Retornos de lo vivo lejano* donde Rafael Alberti se reintegra consigo mismo, aunque con un acento de madurez melancólica, al evocar la infancia y la familia, las habitaciones y los muebles de la casa paterna, las manos de la madre que desgranaban los acordes de agua de la música de Chopin, los días colegiales, las horas de angustia en la ciudad sitiada, los primeros amores, la añoranza de lo perdido para siempre, de lo irreparable, de lo que sólo queda en la memoria y se va difumando con los años hasta desaparecer en las sombras de la muerte. Y estos poemas completan el círculo del retorno que da unidad y cohesión a toda la obra poética de Rafael Alberti.[4]

In *Pleamar* Alberti's recollections of the past are somewhat sketchy, and the reader senses a certain reluctancy on the part of the poet in evoking his past. *Retornos,* on the other hand, makes a conscious attempt at resurrecting some of his most cherished memories. «Retornos de un museo deshabitado» reflects that in his wanderings Alberti actively seeks out those things which will help him in recalling the past:

> Algo me queda siempre cuando estoy solo, cuando emprendiendo el camino del corazón, subiendo las empinadas cuestas de la memoria, elijo de un prado lateral borroso, de una triste sauceda, una vertiente perdida, un separado río de solitarios rumores o una playa, elijo lo que más me revive llamándome.(828)

Alberti likens himself to the naked walls of an abandoned museum which were once covered with treasured works of art:

> Voy de espacio en espacio,
> de vestigio en vestigio,
> de silencio en silencio de señales, recorro
> los inertes cuadrados ciegos, y le pregunto
> a la luz por la vida que los habitó, y lloro
> esperanzado, lloro
> hasta por las profundas cuencas de los oídos.(829).

«Retornos de la dulce libertad» recalls the freedom in exploring new worlds that he possessed as a child. Now that he is older and wiser, he feels that he can once again rediscover these worlds through his poetry:

---

[4] RAFAEL LOZANA, «Apreciación de Rafael Alberti,» *Univ. Caribe,* 25 (Feb. 1960), p. 3.

Podías, cuando fuiste marinero en tierra,
ser más libre que ahora,
yéndote alegremente,
desde las amarradas comarcas encendidas
de tu recién nacido soñar, por los profundos
valles de huertos submarinos, por las verdes
laderas de delfines, sumergidos senderos
que iban a dar a dulces sirenas deseadas.

Libertad, no me dejes. Vuelve a mí, duro y dulce,
como fresca muchacha madurada en la pena.
Hoy mi brazo es más fuerte que el de ayer, y mi canto,
encendido en el tuyo, puede abrir para siempre,
sobre los horizontes del mar nuestra mañana.(851-52)

The poet's longing to relive the past includes a desire to be once again imbued with his former poetic sensitivity. Alberti realizes that his more recent poetry has lacked the visual quality of his earlier work, and in «Retornos de una isla dichosa» he asks to be blessed once again with the ability to perceive things as clearly as before:

Isla de amor, escúchame, antes de que te vayas,
antes, ya que has venido, de que escapes de nuevo:
Concédeme la gracia de aclarar los perfiles
del canto que a mi lengua le quede aún, poniéndole
esa azul y afilada delgadez de contornos
que subes cuando al alba renaces sin rubores,
feliz y enteramente desnuda, de las olas.(827)

It is obvious that this ability is not lost to him. Of all of Alberti's post-Civil War works *Retornos de lo vivo lejano* is the most visual and the richest in color imagery. As Emilia Zuleta points out in her book *Cinco poetas*:

El pasado se corporiza mediante sus elementos accidentales: tras el color se perfila la materia, paisajes, objetos, seres humanos.[5]

«Retornos a través de los colores» demonstrates that color is his closest link with the past:

Esta tarde te alivian los colores: El verde,
aparecido niño grácil de primavera,
el claro mar del cielo que cambia en los cristales
el ala sonreída de un añil mensajero.

Te hacen viajar el blanco tembloroso y erguido
que abren las margaritas contra la enredadera,
el marfil de los senos nacientes del magnolio,
el albo de las calas de pie sobre el estanque.

No pierdes los colores que te juegan caminos
esta tarde en tu breve jardín murado. Mira
aquí están. Tú los tocas. Son los mismos colores
que en tu corazón viven ya un poco despintados.(827-28)

---

[5] EMILIA DE ZULETA, *Cinco poetas españoles* (Madrid: Gredos, 1971), p. 377.

The colors most often employed in *Retornos de lo vivo lejano* are once
again those of his sea. In «Retornos de una mañana de primavera» the
poet exclaims. «Recibe lo que el mar me trajo esta mañana / y suplícale
siempre para mí sus retornos»(821). Alberti's descriptions of the sea are
as vivid as those of *Cal y canto,* and they are decorated with many of the
very same images. The following verse from «Retornos de una mañana
de primavera» reintroduces such popular images as «divina espalda azul» and
«frente de espumas»:

> Quizás con igual número, con la misma incontable
> numeración de olas que desde el nacimiento
> de tu divina espalda azul has conmovido,
> me llamas resonando,
> reventando tu frente de espumas en la orilla
> donde mi luminoso corazón miró siempre,
> mar mío, sobre ti soplar la primavera.(820)

The colors are assigned more or less the same symbolic connotations they
had in *Cal y canto.* The poem just cited is a case in point; the blues and
whites convey innocence, beauty and perfection. The color green in the
following verse is once again associated with hope and life:

> Desde tantas angustias sin eco, desde tantos
> días iguales, noches de un mismo rostro, desde
> las similares cuevas de cada hora, es dulce
> no ofrecer resistencia a tu verde llamada.(820)

Colors and images relating to the sea are most prevalent in the poems
«Retornos del amor.» Here are described the poet's experiences in love.
Of special interest is the physical description of his lover in «Retornos
del amor en medio del mar.» Through a series of sea-related images Alberti presents a vision of his lover which seems to transcend reality:

> Esplendor mío, amor,
> inicial de mi vida,
> quiero decirte toda tu belleza,
> aquí, en medio del mar, cuando voy en tu busca,
> cuando tan sólo puedo compararte
> con la hermosura tibia de las olas.
> Es tu cabeza un manantial de oro,
> una lluvia de espuma dorada que me enciende
> y lleva a navegar al fondo de la noche.
> Es tu frente la aurora con dos arcos
> por los que pasan dulces esos soles
> con que sueñan al alba los navíos.
> ¿Qué decir de tu boca y tus orejas,
> de tu cuello y tus hombros si el mar esconde conchas,
> corales y jardines sumergidos
> que quisieran al soplo
> de las alas del sur ser como ellos?

Son tus costados como dos lejanas
bahías en reposo
donde al son de tus brazos sólo canta
el silencio de amor que las rodea.
Triste es hablar, cuando se está distante,
de los golfos de sombra, de las islas
que llaman al marino que los siente
pasar, sin verlos, fuera de su ruta.
Amor mío, tus piernas son dos playas,
dos médanos tendidos que se elevan
con un rumor de juncos si no duermen.
Dame tus pies pequeños para andarte,
para sentirte todas tus riberas.
Voy por el mar, voy sobre ti, mi vida,
sobre tu amor, hacia tu amor, cantando
tu belleza más bella que las olas.(840-41)

Color is essential in making the association between the two elements which are being compared, the sea and the girl. Most of the color references are direct. For example, gold is specifically mentioned in each of the two images describing the girl's hair: «manantial de oro» and «espuma dorada.» In other images the colors are implied. Her white forehead, for example, is inferred in the word «aurora.» The golden color of her skin is implied in the image, «tus piernas son dos playas.» The sensual colors, pink and red, are alluded to in the description of the woman's more delicate features (her ears, neck, lips, etc.), which the poet compares to the hidden treasures of the sea: shells, coral and undersea gardens.

The colors used in the description of the girl are important in a symbolic sense as well. In addition to the pink, already cited as a symbol of sensuality, blue and white are also used in a symbolic capacity. Blue as mentioned on various occasions, is a symbol of the Ideal, and white, a symbol of purity and innocence. In this and other poems these colors are essential in presenting her as the incarnation of perfection. She is referred to on several occasions as «Venus» or «diosa.» «Retornos del amor entre las ruinas ilustres,» identifies «la diosa» in her abode:

Esta es la casa de la diosa. Aspira
por los azules ámbitos su aroma
a espuma marinera, a los jazmines
y claveles salados de su cuerpo.(844)

«Retornos del amor en los balcones« presents her «cantando»:

Ha pasado la siesta dulce de los azules
que la ancha isla nos tendió en el sueño.
Venus casi dormida aún, te asomas
al íntimo refugio de los barcos
y toda tú ya cantas como un puerto
amoroso de velas y de mástiles.(833)

The colors blue and white accompany all of these references. In «Retornos del amor con la luna,» although the girl is being compared to the moon and not to the sea, a similar sense of purity and perfection is expressed through a series of references to light: «reluciente,» «alumbradoras,» «sol,» «iluminada,» and «dulce luz»:

> Tú eres la luna con la luna. Remontabas
> del fatigado lecho, tan grande y reluciente,
> que las dormidas sábanas oscuras se creían
> ser las alumbradoras de un sol desconocido.
>
> Profunda, era la alcoba como un aljibe inmóvil
> que subiera encantado de un agua iluminada.
> Nadaban sumergidas en dulce luz las ondas
> que tus brazos hacían morir contra los muros.
>
> Cuando al fin ascendías a los altos cristales
> que la luna remota ya con sueño miraba,
> tú, luna con la luna, rebosando, caías
> nuevamente apagada en tu lecho tranquilo.
>
> Otras cosas la luna me trajo en esta noche,
> al subir, solitaria, sobre los mudos árboles.(845)

The description of the girl in the poem «Retornos del amor tal como era» is entirely different from the portrayals admired above. The title of the poem itself implies this difference. The girl depicted therein is not a paragon of perfection surrounded by an aura of purity and innocence, but a woman of flesh and blood who inspires the poet's passionate desires:

> Eras en aquel tiempo rubia y grande,
> sólida espuma ardiente y levantada.
> Parecías un cuerpo desprendido
> de los centros del sol, abandonado
> por un golpe de mar en las arenas.
>
> Todo era fuego en aquel tiempo. Ardía
> la playa en tu contorno. A rutilantes
> vidrios de luz quedaban reducidos
> las algas, los moluscos y las piedras
> que el oleaje contra ti mandaba.
>
> Todo era fuego, exhalación, latido
> de onda caliente en ti. Si era una mano
> la atrevida o los labios, ciegas ascuas,
> voladoras, silbaban por el aire.
> Tiempo abrasado, sueño consumido.
>
> Yo me volqué en tu espuma en aquel tiempo.(833-34)

The girl is still associated with the sea in this poem, but Alberti paints here a sea that has been transformed. «Todo era fuego,» says Alberti. The surf is described as «espuma ardiente,» and the waves as «ondas calientes.» Red and yellow emerge as the predominant colors thereby emphasizing the more passionate and volatile mood.

Retornos de lo vivo lejano is an oasis in the middle of a poetic desert. Though surrounded perhaps by a veil of melancholia, to life once again come colors and images not present in Alberti's world since *Sobre los ángeles,* and which unfortunately are not to be found in any of his subsequent works.

Cuando se va quien se quiere

The theme of nostalgia is presented very differently in *Baladas y canciones del Paraná.* Unlike *Retornos de lo vivo lejano* in which Alberti is able to escape the present and lose himself in his own past, in *Baladas y canciones del Paraná* he is quite conscious of the present. The expansive green pastures, the horses grazing on the land, the weeping willows growing along the river, and the clouds in the sky, all of which could be seen from the poet's balcony which overlooked the river valley below, provide the scenario for the work.

The majority of the poems are nostalgic recollections of the Spanish landscape inspired by the Argentinian panorama. In «Canción # 7» and «# 57» respectively, Alberti states:

> Basta un balcón sobre el río
> y unos caballos paciendo
> para viajar noche y día
> sin moverse.(971)
> ... ...
> El alma de otros paisajes
> se me ha quedado dormida
> en los ojos.(1015)

Even certain smells remind the poet of his homeland: «Con el azahar me voy. / No me detengáis. / Llego a costas que me llaman»(978).

Throughout the book Alberti is drawing comparisons between present and past. All that he sees he attempts to relate to his native Spain. An Argentinian river is «Igual que el Guadalquivir, / o más chico, como el Duero»(1003). The poet says:

> Sé de las islas del mar,
> pero no sé de tus islas.
> Las tuyas tienen caballos,
> niñas azules las mías.(970)

The green pastures are compared to the «mar gaditano»: «Los pastos, como mar verde / del viento que viene y va»(963).

Although there are few references to color in the book they are somewhat unique. The reference to the color of the river as a pale strawberry

at dawn and a ripe strawberry at dusk is an image used for the very
first time in Alberti's poetry:

> Río de Gabato,
> te miro correr.
> Fresa pálido en la mañana.
> Encendido, al atardecer.(999)

Another image which had not previously appeared in the poet's work
is this description of the river as a broken stained glass window:

> Desazogados cristales
> rotos, azules y verdes,
> que no podrá juntar nadie.(1019)

In «Balada del que se creía dormir solo» one finds an interesting variation
of an image Alberti has used before. Without mentioning the color specifically, he describes the thin (green) line of the horizon at dawn as a
serpent hidden beneath a pillow:

> Y una culebra dormida
> debajo de la almohada
> vi en el alba.(975)

«Canción # 13» compares the green pastures to a game table:

> El campo, de terciopelo,
> bordado está de caballos.
> Verde el terciopelo y negra
> la greca de los caballos.(980)

Alberti employs a number of poetic techniques in making his color
references more visually appealing. Personification is featured in «Balada
de Don Amarillo» in describing the parched wheat fields:

> Pobre está Don Amarillo.
> Pobre está.
>
> Pobre a la lluvia y al viento.
> Pobre al sol, Don Amarillo.
> ¡Qué pobre está! (966)

The same technique is applicable to the landscape of Sevilla:

> Pienso en el rey de Sevilla,
> triste y blanco.
>
> Cuelga el río en su cintura
> un alfanje azul de barcos.
> Y encima, el cielo, un turbante
> azul con pájaros blancos.(981)

The golden color of the water in this verse from another poem is an excellent example of an oxymoron:

Beben sol los sauces, beben
el agua helada del sol.(1021)

Color references such as these are few and far between in *Baladas y canciones del Paraná*. But in «Canción # 13» the poet offers a possible explanation for the relative lack of color imagery:

Cuando se va quien se quiere,
el campo se torna oscuro.
No se ve nada, aunque mires,
aunque sepas
que todo está iluminado,
y sepas que las naranjas
siguen de oro, que el río
sigue corriendo de plata,
que sigue el caballo blanco
y negro el cordero negro
y verde el verde del árbol.

Cuando se va quien se quiere,
el campo se torna oscuro
y andas a ciega, buscando.(1022)

Alberti, in reality, has not been abandoned by any one as he suggests in the poem. It is what he himself has left behind that accounts for his sullen and somber mood. Therefore, while color is perhaps not one of the most important elements of *Baladas y canciones del Paraná,* it does play a vital role in the work. Firstly, it is used as an element of comparison in a number of Alberti's descriptions. Secondly, the relative absence of color reflects the poet's own pessimism, boredom and nostalgia.

Thus the poet, in an attempt to relive the past, evokes the element which from the beginning was his basic source of inspiration. The colors of the sea, white, blue and green once again prevail. In *Pleamar* the transparency of the colors along with a series of images which express elusiveness reveal the poet's sense of disorientation and his inability to relate to the past. The more vivid colors and concrete images of *Retornos de lo vivo lejano* reflect a much clearer perspective of the past. Despite the veil of melancholia, Alberti's memories are recalled through images which are as lucid and descriptive as those of *Cal y canto.* In *Baladas y canciones del Paraná* color plays a small but significant role in once again expressing the poet's nostalgia.

Not all of Alberti's post-Civil War poetry focuses on the past. A number of the poems of *Pleamar, Retornos de lo vivo lejano* and *Baladas y canciones del Paraná* are concerned with the poet's future. Alberti reveals in these works that he is no longer a young man, and that he must eventually face the prospect of death. This new and unique side of Alberti is revealed, as we shall see, by the introduction of relatively new colors.

El día que pase el mar

The colors blue, green and white in Alberti's post-Civil War poetry are generally used in reference to the poet's past. To represent the present, the poet choses, instead, colors like yellow, purple, grey and black. While these colors are not alien to Alberti's color scheme, they acquire at times a special significance as we will attempt to show in the following poems.

Traditionally, the color purple is a symbol of anguish and is usually presented in a religious context. During the Easter pageant, for example, it is the symbol of Christ's suffering on the cross. «Es la Pascua,» says Alberti, «purpúrea de la pena»(561). In Alberti's poems the references to the color are usually of a more personal nature. It is the poet's own suffering that he is lamenting when he says:

> Se empurpura la fe, que se entumece
> de nevada sonora,
> de oculto, álgido trigo empurpurado.(561)

Purple is also a symbol of the corruption of innocence. In the following verse from «Púrpura nevada» Alberti writes:

> Hubo un tiempo que dijo, que decía:
> Más blanca que la nieve, prima mía.
> Rosa de Alberti, rosa chica, breve,
> níveamente pintada.
> Hoy diría: Más roja que la nieve,
> ya que la sangre es púrpura nevada.(561)

The color yellow is used more frequently in Alberti's post-Civil War poetry than ever before. Traditionally the color has a variety of connotations but is usually a symbol of poverty, sickness, death and decay. Yellow is also generally associated with autumn, which, in a symbolic sense, is a harbinger of death. «Canción # 3» from *Baladas y canciones del Paraná* refers specifically to the symbolic connotations of the color:

> Amarillos color de la pobreza
> y la desgracia, hermanas amarillas...
>
> Amarillos de otoño, helado umbrío
> que les hiere las manos amarillas.(1017)

Somewhat of a poetic banality or cliché is applied to himself in the autumn of his years. This is expressed quite clearly in «Retornos de una mañana de otoño.» «No es difícil,» says Alberti, «llegar hasta ti sin moverse, / ciudad, ni hasta vosotras, alamedas queridas. / Me basta el amarillo que me cubre y dispone, / difunto, acompañarme adherido a mis pasos»(824). In another verse from the same poem he adds: «Pero la luz se afana por hundirse. Y las hojas / me pesan de llevarlas a cuestas todo el día»(825).

Alberti's fading youth is a theme which is repeated throughout his post-Civil War poetry. «Balada con retornos de Gabriel Miró,» for example, describes the last vestiges of youth as dangling from a thin green string around autumn's neck: «Ahora que el verano, todavía prendido / de un último hilo verde al cuello del otoño»(1041). Alberti accepts somewhat reluctantly the fact that he is growing old:

> Me encontrará la noche llorando esta umbría,
> ya que desde tan lejos me trajo aquí el otoño,
> llorando, sí, llorando,
> porque llegó el momento de gritar que lo estoy
> sobre tantas preciosas ruinas sin remedio.(825)

For the first time in Alberti's poetry, the theme of death is assigned a very personal meaning. The colors black and grey are essential in the construction of images of death. The poet sees omens of death everywhere. The reference to «sombra negra en el verano» in «Canción # 12» stands for one of these many auguries:

> Higueras de la barranca,
> sombra negra en el verano
> hoy arañas del otoño,
> grises, secas.(1021)

«Retornos de una antigua tristeza» makes clear, «un persistente presentimiento oscuro»(853). «Canción # 16» and «# 39» respectively announce:

> Hoy amanecieron negros
> los naranjos.
> Los azahares tan blancos
> ayer a la tarde, negros.
> ¡Qué negros han despertado! (985)
> ... ...
> Me acompaña
> tan sólo la oscuridad.
>
> La más viva oscuridad.(1007)

Despite these rather gloomy apprehensions, Alberti faces the prospect of death with a surprising sense of optimism. His concept of death is somewhat quevedescan. He realizes that death is inevitable and therefore passively accepts it. «Mejor es,» says Alberti, «ya venciéndose el sol por las laderas, / preferir el dorado de las verdes pendientes, / y mejor todavía, / cuando el alma no puede más de otoño y se dobla, / dejarse sin dominio llevar por los declives»(824). Unlike Quevedo Alberti sees the possibility of a life after death which he describes in «Retornos de una dura obsesión» as a light at the end of a long dark road:

> ¡Ah, no poder de pronto empujar tanta noche,
> tantos compactos años de terror y rompiéndolos
> arrebatar al fin esa vedada
> luz que sabes que existe,
> que por saber que existe
> hasta cantando marchas de verdad a la muerte! (853)

The association of darkness with life and light with death is not unique to this poem. In «Retornos de una sombra maldita» Alberti depicts life as a fruit. When we die, says the poet, the pit and bitter peel are removed and what remains is a «corazón sin sombra»:

> ... Que en ese día,
> desnudos de esa amarga corteza, liberados
> de ese hueso de hiel que nos consume,
> alegres, rebosemos
> tu ya tranquilo corazón sin sombra.(851)

«Retornos de Vicente Aleixandre» presents life as a dark sea. Like the tide, death will eventually recede and will make way for a new life:

> Han pasado las cosas. Han caído
> mares de oscuridad, negros telones.
>
> ... Pero mira:
> siempre la muerte retrocede, siempre
> sus yertas oleadas ceden paso
> a esa doliente luz donde se abre,
> niño feliz de espuma azul, la vida.(865)

Despite the tone of finality in a number of the compositions, Alberti never gives up hope of someday returning to his homeland. This verse from «Balada del posible regreso» looms as a prophecy which has since been fulfilled:

> Mi cabeza será blanca,
> y mi corazón tendrá
> blancos también los cabellos
> el día que pase el mar.(987)

As noted, the single most important theme in Alberti's post-Civil War poetry is the poet's nostalgia. While color is instrumental in the development of this theme, it is obvious that it is not the significant element it was in his earlier works. With the possible exception of *Retornos de lo vivo lejano,* Alberti's poems lack the visual quality of his earlier efforts. Shortly after the publication of *Pleamar,* one of the most poorly conceived works from the standpoint of color, Alberti, possibly hoping to capture on canvas what he is no longer able to achieve in his poetry, once again takes up painting. In «Diario de un día» he writes:

En estos últimos meses no me levanto ya para escribir, sino —¡quién lo diría, oh heroicos madrugones de mis tenaces dieciocho años!— para pintar. Poemas, sí. Los míos propios. Para pintarlos solamente. Mi primera y avasalladora vocación me llama hoy, al cabo de casi treinta años de dormida, con una persistencia de la que ya comienzo a tener miedo (780)... ¡Qué redescubrimiento para mí los colores! Paso ahora los días y los días, trasladándolos puros de los tarros, jugándolos ya en líneas gruesas o delgadas por la extensión luminosa del papel. ¡Qué poder de abstracción! ¡Qué medio misterioso de ausentarle, de hacerle a uno viajero feliz de un mundo deslumbrante, del que cuando se regresa se está soñando ya con encontrárselo de nuevo! Mañana, antes aún de que amanezca, me volveré a embarcar, cada vez con más ansia, hacia ese país de los colores, de donde no será difícil que algún día no retorne.(783-84)

The preceding quotation appears to announce his book *A la pintura*, where he pays tribute to an art form, which, from the time he began writing, had a significant effect on his poetry.

Chapter V

A la pintura

As our study has revealed, Alberti demonstrates throughout his work a profound knowledge of the techniques generally associated with the visual arts. Nevertheless, it is not until we read his book *A la pintura* that we realize how knowledgeable of and sensitive to art Alberti really is. In her article «Pintura y poesía en Rafael Alberti» Ana María Winkelman describes this work as the poetic culmination of his sincere interest in painting.[1] Fernando Quiñones sees *A la pintura* more as a study than a lyrical work. In his article «Tres toques rápidos a la poesía de Rafael Alberti» he states:

> A mí *A la pintura* me parece «un trabajo» más que un libro de poesía propiamente dicho; un trabajo magnífico, eso sí, pero trabajo, o si lo queréis así, una espléndida guía en verso «de» y «para» la pintura (más que «a» la pintura), con mucho de homenaje.[2]

Quiñones' argument is, in our opinion, unfounded and somewhat self-contradictory. He agrees that the work has «mucho de homenaje,» but, denies that the title «*A*» *la pintura* appropriately befits its contents. The book does very clearly reveal Alberti's knowledge on the subject of art; on the other hand, it seems doubtful that the poet's intentions were didactic. One is more inclined to concur with Eduardo González Lanuza who, in his «Homenaje a Rafael Alberti,» defends *A la pintura* on the basis of its poetic merits:

> Así asistimos al trabajo de Alberti en su taller en su doble vocación, pero en un juego donde el pintor se entrega muy felizmente a la superior capacidad realizadora del poeta.[3]

The character of *A la pintura* is generally approbatory. Alberti gives the impression that he personally acknowledges what art has meant for him. Many of the poems begin with the vocative «A ti,» which, as Ana María Winkelman points out, adds a humanizing touch even to the most abstract poems.[4] Not all of the compositions, however, are complimen-

---

[1] Ana María Winkelman, «Pintura y poesía en Rafael Alberti,» *Papeles de Son Armadans,* 30 (1963), p. 162.

[2] Fernando Quiñones, «Tres toques rápidos a la poesía de Rafael Alberti,» *Cuadernos Hispanoamericanos,* 53 (1963), p. 527.

[3] Eduardo González Lanuza, «Crónicas: Homenaje a Rafael Alberti,» *Sur,* X (1941), p. 56.

[4] Ana María Winkelman, pp. 151-152.

tary. Alberti does show a preference for certain painters and styles, and this preference is clearly revealed in the spirit of the poems themselves. Among those painters Alberti admires most are Pablo Picasso, to whom the edition of *A la pintura*, which we will be examining, is dedicated, and Raul Soldi, who painted a portrait of Alberti's daughter Aitana, and of whom he writes:

> Tenías que ser tú, pintor, gracia liviana,
> música diluida,
> luz vaporosa, frágil, desasida,
> quien pintase en el aire puro el aire de Aitana.(707-08)

Alberti's distaste for the work of such painters as Valdés Leal and Gutiérrez Solana is equally obvious. He refers to Valdés Leal as, «pintor de la nada»(675). Alberti describes Solana's work as:

> La beatería
> más sombría
> con su temblor de perlesía:
> la mayúscula porquería.(699)

A la pintura is concerned primarily with painting. There are, however, references throughout the work to related art forms such as sculpture and line drawing. The poems of *A la pintura* are devoted to a variety of topics. There is a series of thirty or so brief poetic impressions on each of six colors: blue, red, yellow, green, black and white. A number of rigidly constructed sonnets treat certain artistic techniques and elements related to art: the hand, crayon, pallet, retina, line, perspective, claroscuro, movement, nudity, garb, color, light, shadow, watercolor, artistic taste and divine proportion. Lastly, there are a number of poems dedicated to certain artists. Unlike the rigidly constructed sonnets, these poems have no form in particular. Their structure, rather, is derived from the content of the poems themselves. One of the best examples is the poem «El Bosco» whose «staccato» rhythm and vulgar language gives us more or less the same impression we would get upon seeing the artist's own paintings. Ana María Winkelman believes that there are six artists whose work represents for Alberti a synthesis of art. In her opinion, Leonardo Da Vinci stands for beauty, knowledge and artistic restraint. Verones' work is an expression of vitality and life. El Greco is the master of contrast, movement and light, and his work reflects a certain mystical anguish. Rubens is the epitome of sensualism; Goya, a master of sensationalism and the grotesque; Picassso, the prime exponent of subjectivity in art. Miss Winkelman's summary is difficult to accept in its totality. It seems apparent that Alberti intended the work as a whole to be a synthesis of art, a concept that must be faithfully considered if one does not wish to err. There are a number of artists not included in the list of the six mentioned above. Velázquez, for example, is perhaps the best exponent of realism. Alberti is quite concise on this trait:

Se apareció la vida una mañana
y le suplicó:
—Píntame, retrátame
como soy realmente o como tú
quisieras realmente que yo fuese.(669)

Rafael's paintings reveal a certain sensitivity which is unique only to him. Rembrandt and Miguel Angel, not El Greco, are the names Alberti most often associates with contrast and light. Renoir, Gauguin and Renato Guttoso are set apart for their treatment of color. For in Guttoso «Ya el arco-iris canta en la tormenta»(713); in Gauguin «El color / de viaje, / se hizo aroma de flor / perfume de paisaje / isla, amor»(694); and in Renoir:

Los colores soñaban. ¡Cuánto tiempo,
oh, cuánto tiempo hacía!
El rosa era quien quería
resbalar por el seno y ser cadera.
El amarillo, cabellera.
La cabellera, rosas amarillas.
El añil, diluirse entre los muslos
y ceñir hecho agua las rodillas.
El plata, ser olivo
y vino de clavel el rojo vivo.
¿Se murió el color negro?
El azul es, quien canta
y se destila
en una sombra verde y lila.(689)

Finally, the one painter most often mentioned with regard to movement in art is Van Gogh who is

Fuente
de aparente
corriente
desordenada.(695)
... ...
Se arremolina,
campesina,
ondula.
Noche en círculo rueda,
azula
la arboleda.(695)

There are a number of editions of *A la pintura*. Since the primary concern of our study, however, is color, we have chosen to comment upon one particular illustrated edition of this work. The book in question is the 1968 edition published by Aguilar in the «Colección La Arboleda.» It includes a prologue by Vicente Aleixandre, a dedication to Pablo Picasso and 95 illustrations (most of which are color photographs of paintings) which enable the reader to visualize the color references in Alberti's poems.

The first poem, which is entitled simply «1917,» reveals exactly how much of an effect painting actually had on Alberti's poetry. The poem recalls Alberti's introduction to formal art in the Prado Museum as well as his own frustrated desire to become a painter:

> ... la ilusión de soñarme siquiera un olvidado
> Alberti en los rincones del Museo del Prado;
> la sorprendente, agónica, desvelada alegría
> de buscar la Pintura y hallar la Poesía,
> con la pena enterrada de enterrar el dolor
> de nacer un poeta por morirse un pintor,
> hoy distantes me llevan, y en verso remordido,
> a decirte ¡Oh Pintura! mi amor interrumpido.(615)

From the poem we learn that many of the poetic references we have discussed in relation to Alberti's other works could have stemmed from his interest in art. The little green siren often encountered in Alberti's work, for example, could have grown out of his admiration for the sirens in the Rubens' paintings he saw in the Prado:

> Las sirenas de Rubens, sus ninfas aldeanas
> no eran las ruborosas deidades gaditanas
> que por mis mares niños e infantiles florestas
> nadaban virginales o bailaban honestas.(613)

Alberti's approach to many of the mylthological themes is very possibly a direct result of the way in which these themes are presented in the works of the famous masters:

> Y me bañé de Adonis y Venus juntamente
> y del líquido rostro de Narciso en la fuente.(614)

The greatest contribution of painting on Alberti's work, however, is the poet's understanding and appreciation of color not only as an artistic device, but as a poetic device as well. Alberti explains that he was initially attracted to the Impressionists because of the clarity of their colors. As Angel Crespo points out in his article «Realismo y pitagorismo,» Alberti's own references to color are in line with the precepts of the impressionists. Crespo refers specifically to the way Alberti employs certain verbs, nouns and adjectives which suggest light:

> El color *alumbra* al árbol, las flores son comas *radiantes,* el agua discos *transparentes,* el bermellón *arde,* el naranja es *luminoso,* el verde cromo *empalidece,* el *sol* aquilata al blanco, la *luz* llueve, la hora es *clarificada* azul y, en fin, el *ojo* es nombrado en el poema en su función indagatoria.[5]

There are, as we mentioned earlier, six colors Alberti is primarily

---

[5] ANGEL CRESPO, «Realismo y pitagorismo en el libro de Alberti *A la pintura,*» *Papeles de Son Armadans,* XXX (1963), p. 99.

concerned with in *A la pintura*: blue, red, yellow, green, black and white. There is also a fairly wide range of hues, most of which remain undefined and can only be visualized within the context of certain paintings. The way these colors are presented, however, is for the most part, the same way they are exposed throughout Alberti's work. In this way *A la pintura* is not only a synthesis of art, but a synthesis of Alberti's own use of color as well. Many of the same color images we discussed in reference to some of Alberti's other works are used in reference to specific painters and their works. In some cases they are taken out of context and presented as poetic impressions or vignettes.

The most prominent color in *A la pintura* is blue. In fact, in his article «Gracia, misterio y nostalgia de Rafael Alberti,» Eduardo Carranza seems to emphasize a particular shade of blue in his description of the book. He calls it, «Libro denso, luciente, transparente, hondo de hondura mágica y verde-azul.»[6]

The color blue is applied here much in the same way as it is used in Alberti's other work. Most often it is associated with the sea. In his poem to Picasso, for example, Alberti describes:

> Málaga.
>
> Azul, blanco y añil
> postal y marinero.
> De azul se arrancó el toro del toril,
> de azul el toro del chiquero.
> De azul se arrancó el toro.
> ¡Oh guitarra de oro,
> oh toro por el mar, toro y torero! (700)

The other common association of the color blue with the sky is also repeated throughout the book. In the poem «Miguel Angel» we find the following description:

> Atrás, rompiendo, aplastadora, inmune,
> salta la arquitectura, blanco cíclope
> furioso, en el azul tendiendo arcos,
> subiendo fustes al frontón del cielo,
> bajo el ojo asombrado de las cúpulas.(632)

The color retains the same symbolic values as well. We mentioned earlier that blue is traditionally the color of the Ideal. It connotes beauty, purity, perfection and a certain sense of elusiveness. In this context, Alberti often associates blue with the Virgin Mary: «Trajo su virginal azul la Virgen: / azul María, azul Nuestra Señora»(624). A similar application is found in the poem to «Corot,» the French Impressionist: «Pintor de la sonrisa feliz y del aliento / desfallecido de los humos vagos, / silfo del bosque, morador del viento, / hilo azul de la Virgen de los lagos»(684).

Alberti singles out a number of painters for their use of the color

---

[6] EDUARDO CARRANZA, «Gracia, misterio y nostalgia de Rafael Alberti,» *Boletín Cultural y Bibliográfico*, X (1967), p. 134.

blue. In the poem «Leonardo,» blue is the only color specifically mentioned:

> Volar, volar, pero sabiendo el ojo
> que no hay pájaro o flecha que lo engañen,
> perspectivas celestes que las torres
> con su mentira azul lo descarríen.
> Sueño de la pupila que no sueña.(623)

Of Poussin Alberti writes:

> Roma de los azules Poussin entre los pinos.(625)

The poet adds:

> En la paleta de Velázquez tengo
> otro nombre: me llamo Guadarrama.(625)

Other painters mentioned for their use of the color blue include El Greco, Giotto, Tintoretto, Rubens, Tiépolo, Goya, Manet, Titian and Renoir. But Picasso, receives the greatest distinction for his utilization of blue:

> Picasso:
> maternidad azul, arlequín rosa.(701)
> ... ...
> Dijo el azul un día:
> —Hoy tengo un nuevo nombre. Se me llama:
> Azul Pablo Ruiz Azul Picasso.(627)

The works Alberti singles out as prime examples of the use of the color blue in art are Picasso's «The Tragedy,» from the painter's blue period, Fra Angelico's «The Anunciation,» Boticelli's «Birth of Venus,» and two of Giotto's works, «The Virgin of all the Saints» and «The Adoration».

The color red encompasses, perhaps, a great deal more in the way of hues than does the color blue. Alberti chooses to include such color variations as purple, violet, pink and orange within the range of reds. Among those poetic vignettes included in the series entitled «Al rojo» are the following:

> El púrpura a través de los cristales
> —copa, vaso, botella—
> calientes de los vinos.(639)
> ... ...
>
> Pierdo el sentido en rosa,
> hasta desvanecerme en casi blanco.(640)
> ... ...
>
> Ven, amarillo. Quiero ser naranja,
> cadmio lustroso esférico entre el verde.(639)

This color, in all its variations and hues, is used in reference to specific artists and their works. The bright rich red or crimson, traditionally a symbol of hate, fear, passion and war, characterizes the works of Durero, Rubens, Breughel and Bosch:

> Soy el infierno —Brueghel,
> Bosch— y el nocturno espanto
> en los ojos insomnes de los niños.(638)
> ... ...
> El rojo recortado
> —Flandes— hasta llegar
> —Rubens— al derramado de la orgía.(639)
> ... ...
> Todo es prueba de fuego
> métrica tinta en llama.(648)

The deeper, almost purple, shade of red which evokes anguish and suffering, is alluded to in reference to El Greco's paintings:

> Me levanto hasta el solio de la púrpura
> y desciendo esparcido —¡Oh Greco!— en pliegues.(639)

The soft pink, a symbol of sensuality, is mentioned with respect to the works of such painters as Renoir, and Picasso:

> Me vertí en rosa —Renoir— y puse
> un nuevo nombre —Renoir— al mío.(640)
> ... ...
> Bajé hasta el rosa rosa de Picasso.(640)

The paintings Alberti selects as those which best depict the use of the color red in art are Rafael's «The Cardinal,» and Monet's «Poppy field.» The many variations of red (the range of flesh tones, pink, purple, violet, etc.) can be seen in such paintings as Rafael's «The Virgen of the Curtain,» Titian's «Venus of the Wolf-pup (sic.),» Picasso's «The Lovers» and Delacroix's «The Death of Sardanapolous.»

The color with perhaps the widest range of symbolic possibilities is yellow. Alberti sees it as both a symbol of happiness as well as a symbol of poverty, sickness, death and decay:

> Cuando rompo a volar y mi garganta
> suelta un oro de flautas repetidas,
> le dan a mi alegría un amarillo:
> Amarillo canario.(652)
> ... ...
> Me llamo lividez, entumecido
> exangüe cadavérico estirado.(651)

As we mentioned in our last chapter, the color is often associated with

113

autumn. The toll that time has taken on nature is marked by a change in color from green to yellow:

> Mas tengo el privilegio de ser verde
> y desnudarme —otoño— en amarillo.(649)

Yellow is also used to describe the effect of time on other objects such as a sheet of paper, «Seca piel de arrugado pergamino»(650), or the ivory keyboard of a piano, «Esqueleto y sonora dentadura / luciente de los claves y pianos»(651).

Alberti's references to the use of the color yellow in art reflect the great disparities in its symbolic connotations. Van Gogh and Goya represent to Alberti the more positive values of the color. Alberti is no doubt referring to Goya's earlier works such as «The Parasol» and «Blindman's Bluff» when he writes:

> Amarillo descarga, amarillento
> estampido, lujoso y claro, en Goya.(652)
> ... ...
> Sueno, resueno, grito
> hasta hincarme en el centro
> —Van Gogh— de la retina y desgarrarla.(653)

The pale yellow, symbol of death and decay, is most vividly captured in the paintings of El Greco:

> Sonámbulo, espectral, aparecido,
> cálido, turbio —Greco—, pantanoso,
> gélido, indigestado, vomitado,
> diluido, llovido, evaporado,
> difunto, corrompido, disecado,
> vivo, resucitado...(651)

Alberti also associates the color with the richness and grandeur of the art of the Middle Ages:

> Oro en el nimbo de los viejos santos.
> Oro ingenuo labrado de Edad Media.(649)

The painter that Alberti singles out for his use of yellow is Titian:

> Todo se dora. El siena que en lo umbrío
> cuece la selva en una luz tostada
> dora el ardor del sátiro cabrío
> tras de la esquiva sáfira dorada;
> y un rubio viento, umbrales y dinteles,
> basamentos, columnas, capiteles.(637)

The two paintings which accompany the poems in the series entitled «Amarillo» are Toulouse-Lautrec's «The Clowness Cha-u-kao» and Vincent Van Gogh's «Sunflowers».

Next to blue, the color most often mentioned in the work is green. The color has a variety of traditional as well as very personal symbolic connotations. Like yellow, there are great disparities in the symbolic connotations of the color green. Recognizing these disparities, Alberti explains:

> Claro, soy la Esperanza.
> Pero me descompongo y tengo entonces
> cierto horrible matiz: el verde Envidia.(659)

Generally the color green is associated with Springtime, the sea and nature. «Tengo otro nombre siempre: Primavera»(659). Similar references include: «Y alta forma de copa, que los árboles / se encargan presurosos de llenar, / hasta el borde, de verde»(659); and «Mi forma repetida más constante, / desde que vi la luz, es la de hoja»(659) . . . «Yo soy el verdemar, / subido a azul cuando el azul del cielo / tiende su pecho azul sobre mi espalda»(658).

Finally, there is a rather unique and highly personal, symbolic connotation attached to the color green. In a number of poems it is associated with the past, and thus becomes the color of the poet's nostalgia: «Un verde sumergido en las aguas del tiempo»(659). . . . «Y un verde, el más hermoso / de los verdes, que olvido o no recuerdo»(663). Green is mentioned in reference to nearly every painter in the book: Tintoretto, Brueghel, Titian, Veronés, El Greco, Velázquez, Rembrandt, Rubens, Goya, Delacroix, Courbet, Cézanne, Manet, Sisley, Pissarro, and Renoir. Alberti refers to the green in Goya's paintings as, «un verde popular de romería»(662); to Brueghel's paintings as «El alegre, bailable, florecido / verde —Brueghel— flamenco»(660).

He describes Rembrandt's work with «Voz de verde misterio»(661); and El Greco's paintings, replete with:

> Un agónico verde helado Greco,
> un verde musgo legamoso Greco,
> un disecado verde vidrio Greco,
> un verde roto Greco.(661)

The transparent, almost liquid quality of the color green in the works of the French Impressionists is mentioned on a number of occasions:

> A ti, verde lavado,
> líquido verde Francia
> (Manet, Sisley, Monet,
> Pissarro, Renoir...).(662)
> ... ...
> Me lavaron también, me evaporaron
> pinceles que a la luz pidieron todo.(662)

The color of the sea in Tintoretto's paintings appears as a dense, deep green:

> El mar vomita un verde umbroso alga
> que al expandirse inunda,
> tomándola por playa,
> la tenebrosa luz que empuja al Tintoretto.(661)

There is even a hint of green in the veins of the mythological characters of Rubens' paintings:

...ese caballo que se desborda en hombre,
hinchándole las venas el verde soplo extraño
de erigirse en los tuétanos de la mar como tromba
que lo mueve, lo empuja, lo exalta y lo eterniza.(655)

Paintings which illustrate the use of the color green in art include
Cezanne's «The Bridge of Maincy,» Picasso's «Lady in Green,» and
Poussin's «The Summer» and «Midas and Bacchus.»

In the series of poetic impressions dedicated to the color black possible
visual and symbolic characteristics of the color are numerous. Alberti
associates black with night: «Negro como la boca de la noche»(677);
with the sea: «Un túmulo de negras sombras, un imponente / manto en
caído mar negro del Greco»(678); with caverns and mines: «El negro
misterioso, secreto, de las minas»(680); with fire: «El alma negra junto
al rojo, en llamas»(680); with death: «Monumento callado de la muerte»(679); with pride: «Fui en el retrato majestad y orgullo»(679); and,
ironically, even with happiness: «Un negro como flor de la alegría»(678).

While Alberti alludes to the color black in reference to a number of
painters (Goya, Rembrandt, Velázquez, Titian, Carreño, Zurbarán, Braque,
Gris, Manet and Picasso), he singles out: Ribera, «Negro negro Ribera
negro negro»(679) and Goya's «Aquelarre,» an excellent example to evoke
feelings of mystery, horror, fear and death generally associated with the
color.

The role of white is dramatized in the series of thirty three different
and ingenious vignettes entitled «Blanco» where it is assigned to a variety
of objects as reflected in the examples that follow:

Yo vi —Rafael Alberti—
la luz entre los blancos populares.(690)
... ...

Blanco como la nieve, blanco como
el papel, blanco blanco
como la cal al sol
de los tranquilos muros andaluces.(690)
... ...

Mi infancia fue un rectángulo
de cal fresca, de viva
cal con mi alegre solitaria sombra.(691)
... ...

Yo soy el hijo de la cal más pura.(691)
... ...

Soy el más albañil de los colores.(691)
... ...

Espuma de la mar, galopadora.(692)
... ...

De pronto caigo como traje o nube.(692)
... ...

Soy mantel, alba, níveo
encaje en el cristal de las heladas.(692)

The symbolic connotations of the color are rather limited. As such it is primarily assigned to purity and innocence:

> Blanco puro, total, mas prisionero
> en un cuadrado, un círculo, un triángulo.(694)

Very often it has a somewhat spiritual or mystical quality:

> Blanco de aparición, blanco del éxtasis.(693)

White is the color Alberti generally associates with Cádiz. In a sense, it becomes the color of the poet's own childhood innocence: «Blanco Cádiz de plata en el recuerdo»(691).

The color white has a very special function in art. When combined with other colors, it lightens them. Alberti alludes to this particular characteristic of the color throughout the book:

> Dijo el blanco: —Yo puedo,
> feliz, estar en todo, porque soy
> la imprescindible sangre para el justo
> clarear de la luz en los colores.(690)
> ... ...
>
> Soleo, aclaro, enturbio,
> diluyo, transparento,
> lavo, esfumo, evaporo...(693)
> ... ...
>
> Pierdo el sentido en rosa,
> hasta desvanecerme en casi blanco.(640)
> ... ...
>
> Hay paletas celestes como alas
> descendidas del blanco de las nubes.(624)

The color white without preference for any one, is associated with a number of artists: Zurbarán, El Greco, Piero della Francesca, Uccello, Brueghel, Tintoretto, and many of the French Impressionists. He tells Tintoretto and Brueghel respectively:

> Hubiera yo querido
> sentirme por tu cólera
> hendido, sacudido,
> y en medio del paisaje
> fluvial, por la hermosura
> de la virgen sin traje
> que prolonga en el agua su blancura.(642)
> ... ...
>
> Blanco toca tirante recortado.
> Blanco nieve de Brueghel, campesino.(693)

For Alberti, the paintings that best illustrate the use of white as an

117

artistic tool are Zurbarán's «San Serapio,» Manet's «Bouquet of Peonies and Scissors,» and Gauguin's «The White Horse.»

Although Alberti dedicates respectively one poem (composed of variegated short stanzas) to black and white, it is more common, both in this work as well as in his other collections, to find these colors juxtaposed and not utilized alone. The blackboard image is perhaps one of the more familiar examples of the juxtaposition of black and white:

> Una línea, una letra,
> un rayón, solamente en blanco tiza
> sobre el terso nocturno mudo de los *(sic)* pizarras.(691)

An interesting variation on this image is the following reference to the black ink on a white sheet of paper:

> Una línea, una letra
> sobre mí.   ¡Inolvidable maravilla!(691)

One of the more dramatic uses of this «bi-color» is the artistic technique known as the «claroscuro» or the struggle between light and dark.

> Dio su revés la luz.   Y nació el negro.(677)

In another poem he remarks:

> Negro como la boca de la noche,
> como boca de lobo, como abismo
> sin fin, como agujero
> que recortan los cuerpos en algunas
> determinadas claras superficies.(677-78)

As in *Sobre los ángeles,* the poet seems to create a struggle between light and dark resembling a real battle among fighting men where wounds are common and deep. In the following verse, for example, one finds such words as «herido,» «arrebatado,» «combatiente,» and «ofensor»:

> A ti nocturno, por la luz herido,
> luz por la sombra herida de repente;
> arrebatado, oscuro combatiente,
> claro ofensor de súbito ofendido.(655)

To fortify himself with the «claroscuro» ammunition, he seeks the aid of Zurbarán, Goya, and the master producer of this tool Rembrandt whom he visits in his «taller»:

> A la luz se le abrió, se le dio entrada
> en los más hondos sótanos.
> Y allí una misteriosa
> voz le ordenó de súbito: ¡Combate,
> batalla hombro con hombro, aliento con aliento,
> contra el bostezo helado de las sombras!(655-56)

«Claroscuro» in art is exemplified in Picasso's bullfight sketches done in pen and ink, in Rembrandt's «Self Portrait,» Goya's «The Pilgrimage of San Isidro,» and Valdés Leal's «Postrimerías.»

It can safely be stated that the employment of colors in *A la pintura* runs the gamut of emotional and pictorial effects which are deeply and sincerely experienced by the poet. His ability to handle color technique which in this work is found in a superlative degree, is also evident, though in scattered examples, in the other works treated. Alberti's skills as a painter and his profound knowledge of the concepts of art are effectively and uniquely articulated in his poetry.

Conclusion

Rafael Alberti is certainly one of the more visually oriented poets of the «Generation of 1927.» Because of Alberti's concern for external symbols, Luis Felipe Vivanco defines his poetry as, «la palabra más felizmente superficial de toda la poesía española contemporánea.»[1] Through his work Alberti reveals that he is cognizant of and responsive to shapes, forms and especially color. Our poet's colors are seldom found in isolated references. They appear intricately woven among a network of images within a rigid framework composed of one or more of the principal elements: fire, earth, air and water.

Generally speaking, the elements retain their traditional symbolic connotations in Alberti's poetry. While earth, for example, is usually a negative element which symbolizes restraint and even death, Alberti often casts her (earth) in a traditional mother image symbolic of warmth and shelter. Water most often represents life, and, as we have seen, the sea has an heroic role in Alberti's poetry. Air suggests freedom, elusiveness and creativity. Fire is symbol of passion and surging emotions, although there are a number of allusions to the purging effect of the element. The fusion of two or more of these elements in a particular work often results in highly symbolic interpretations, almost always, however, along traditional lines.

The colors usually retain their traditional symbolic connotations if it can be said that there are, in fact, traditional color symbols. But because Alberti's color images are derived from his own inventiveness and experiences, they very often have strong personal meanings as well. The little green mermaid from *Marinero en tierra* and the post-Civil War image of Spain as the hide of a bull stretched out over a sea of blood are two examples which clearly reflect the personal nature of color imagery in Alberti's poetry. In this study we have attempted to show how the development of certain color patterns throughout Alberti's work reflects the poet's changing moods. The chronological presentation of his works clearly reveals the affinity with the four elements stated previously. The duality land/sea, as we have seen, provides the framework for the study of Alberti's first three works: *Marinero en tierra. La amante* and *El alba*

---

[1] Luis Felipe Vivanco, «Rafael Alberti en su palabra acelerada y vestida de luces» in *Introducción a la poesía española contemporánea* (Madrid: Guadarrama, 1961), p. 228.

del alhelí. The dominant element of *Marinero* is clearly the sea while *El alba...* is dedicated almost exclusively to the land. *La amante* functions as transitional work. There is also a significant shift in the poet's color scheme. In *Marinero en tierra* the dominant colors are white, blue and green. Red is of some importance, while black is used primarily as an element of contrast. *La amante* is mainly garbed in green. *El alba del alhelí* is dominated by black along with green and white. In the two latter works blue seems to have less appeal in Alberti's color scheme, except in his descriptions of the northern coast in *La amante* where one finds significant variations in the application of the color. The change in the poet's color scheme reflects a marked tendency away from the childlike happiness and innocence of *Marinero en tierra,* and a growing concern for the mundane.

There is a significant and somewhat abrupt change in the elemental framework of Alberti's two subsequent works. Air and fire replace water and earth as the dominant elements. This change is reflected in the poet's mood. Alberti becomes very introspective, and his poetry offers a far more subjective view of life. The gradual evolution that takes place in the poet's color scheme from *Marinero en tierra* through *El alba del alhelí* continues until finally in *Cal y canto* the colors begin to diverge, and there emerges an ambience characteristic of polar regions. The blues and whites now add to the overall sense of structured beauty and perfection. The reds and blacks reveal a more or less subconscious desire for violence and destruction. In *Sobre los ángeles* the polar-like peculiarities become even more pronounced. All is reduced to black and white. A personal crisis, which the poet is undergoing at the time, is depicted in this work through a number of contrasting elements, the most obvious of which is the struggle between light and dark.

Another very real crisis, the Spanish Civil War, marks a turning point in Alberti's poetry. The unstable political situation in Spain brings Alberti out of his introspectiveness, and he begins to see things objectively once again.

Alberti's post-Civil War poetry is notably inferior in quality to his previous work. His attempts at developing new themes often result in insipid poems about his dog and his daughter. To recover the seemingly lost thread of poetic inspiration, he is once again forced to look to his past. A definite break in the poet's color scheme results. Early color patterns begin to repeat themselves, but not as noticeably as in his earlier work. His images also lack the imagination and visual force which once characterized them. In *Pleamar* Alberti tries to recreate the environment of *Marinero en tierra* by consciously employing many of the same colors he had used in this first collection of poems. The blues, greens and whites appear faded, however, almost transparent. This unique color consistency along with the introduction of a number of images which suggest fugacity, tend to emphasize the poet's sense of disorientation as well as his remoteness from those innocent and carefree days of childhood. *Retornos de lo vivo lejano* is a more objective and concrete look at the poet's past. By the time Alberti begins writing the poems included in this work, it is obvious that he has formulated a clearer perspective on life which is reflected in the preciseness of the color images he employs. Some of the poems of *Pleamar, Retornos de lo vivo lejano,* and *Baladas y canciones del Paraná* reveal to a greater degree the poet's concern for the future than for the past. This is apparent in the introduction of relatively new colors like yellow and gold which are in themselves symbolic of the poet's mellowing years. In these works, death manifests itself for the first time as a major theme.

As the poet gets older, the visual effects which had characterized his work become less pronounced; they are almost negligible in his most recent works. Shortly after the publication of *Pleamar,* Alberti reverts to painting, a hobby he had cultivated as a child. His sudden renewed interest in this art might be explained as either a disinterest in evoking, or an incapacity to achieve the markedly visual character of his earlier poems. Alberti's book, *A la pintura* is the poet's own monument in verse to an art form he loved and understood, and which had a significant influence on his poetry.

Among the many themes considered tangential to our main stream of color, is his consideration of bullfighting. Through his application of color, Alberti brings to life a moving spectacle and symbolically applies it to Spain as a whole. Here symbols and images drenched principally with red hues express the tragedy of Spain and the poet's melancholy.

Principally, Alberti seems to be fond of two methods of injecting color and color images: by directly naming, positioning and connecting the adjective with the noun it modifies or affects, and by using the object or noun itself whose consistency or nature serves for the color needed. Among the many examples cited, for instance, the sea was a «sábana azul, con embozo / de espumas blancas y amenas»(108); it was also described as «murallas azules»(76). Such nouns as «nieve,» «yelo,» «mármol,» «marfil,» «jazmín,» «Cal» and «confitero» supplied his white; «grana,» «rubí» and «sangre,» red; «carbón,» «sombra,» «tumba» and «cueva,» black; «añil» and «marino,» blue; and «huerto» and «vergel,» green.

Another technique extensively employed by the poet is the vision. Many times we see that the dawn is envisioned as a woman's body. Images seemingly unrelated to either the dawn or a woman's body are used in drawing the association between the two: «mármoles mudos, deshelados»(199); «líquido mármol de alba y pluma»(199); «tus marfiles ondulados»(201); «los jazmines y claveles salados de su cuerpo»(844).

At this point, it can be said that limited contacts with Alberti's poetry may produce the impression that the poet is familiar with colors and their use. But how skillfully and extensively he applies them and how adept he is in knowing their most artistic effects is not always discernible. However, now that several of his works have been subjected in this study to a planned scrutiny, Alberti emerges as a «poet-painter» conscious of the potential of colors and color images in all aspects of nature. In his hand, color is a powerful tool used almost without limits to enhance a multitude of moods, images and artistic effects.

Another point that might be made with respect to Alberti's conscious use of color is his association with the Vanguard movements in Europe. This interest seems to lead his poetry into abstract imagery. Nevertheless, he very calculatingly uses color in order to provide the reader with something tangible, thus enabling him to grasp otherwise difficult images.

We can safely say, therefore, that whether Alberti uses color decoratively or symbolically, he is certainly aware of what he is doing. There are few, if any, random references to color which do not fit into Alberti's elaborately patterned color scheme. Alberti's poetry is not superficial and does not lack depth and sensivity as judged at times. The poet is conscious of his work. He values external symbols such as color and form and visually uses them to represent some of his innermost feelings. Alberti seems to strike an ideal balance between form and essence. He treats and decorates the elements of nature, land and sea, air and fire, with the skilled hand of the consummate artist who is sensitive to the power of creation. Aspects of nature's grandeur and her turbulence are brought to life as they exist and as they are envisioned; and the poet reacts to them with his own moods to sense at different times ugliness and beauty, despair and hope, indifference and love. Lorenzo Varela sums up Alberti's poetry fairly accurately when he says, «Es Rafael Alberti un ejemplo de lealtad a la belleza, de conciencia y responsabilidad en el oficio de poeta. Su poesía revela una unidad de inteligencia y corazón, de razón y pasión.»[2]

---

[2] LORENZO VARELA, «La flauta y el pito; el tambor y el salmo; y la poesía (en torno a Rafael Alberti),» *Tall,* II (1940), No. 10, p. 45.

SELECTED BIBLIOGRAPHY

ADAMS, Hazard. *The Contexts of Poetry.* Boston: Little Brown and Co., 1963.

ALBERTI, Rafael. *A la pintura.* Madrid: Aguilar, 1968.

— «Algo sobre Jazmín, alma errante de Punta del Este.» *La Nación* (3 April 1949).

— «Andalucía,» *La Prensa,* San Juan, 2 (1959).

— «Andalucía, velero siempre deseado.» *La Nación* (31 Oct. 1959).

— «Antonio Machado.» *Hora,* Santiago de Chile (13 Nov. 1945).

— *La Arboleda perdida.* 2nd ed., Buenos Aires: Compañía General Fabril Editora, 1959.

— *La Arboleda perdida* (libro primero de memorias). México: Séneca, 1942.

— «Antonio Bonet, arquitecto mediterráneo.» *Revista Nacional de Cultura,* 13 (1952).

— «Autocrítica: 'El hombre deshabitado'.» *ABC* (19 Feb. 1931).

— «Cuando Machado dejó Madrid.» *España Republicana,* Buenos Aires (19 July 1945).

— «Desde las playas y los bosques.» *Tiempo* (20 March 1952).

— «Diario de un día.» *Universidad Nacional de Colombia,* 17 (Sept. 1953).

— «Don Francisco de Quevedo: poeta de la muerte.» *Revista Nacional de Cultura,* 22 (1960), pp. 140-141.

— «Don Manuel de Falla.» *Tiempo* (10 Feb. 1952).

— «Una égloga y tres paisajes.» *Sed,* Buenos Aires, 1 (1944).

— «Federico García Lorca en Sevilla.» *El Heraldo,* Caracas (17 Nov. 1941).

— «Federico en Sevilla.» *Saber Vivir,* Buenos Aires, 2 (1941).

— «Federico García Lorca y la Residencia de Estudiantes.» *Revista de las Indias,* Bogotá, 30 (1941).

— «Homenaje que ofrecen a Picasso.» *Sur,* Málaga, El Guadalhorce, 1966.

— «Imagen de Federico García Lorca.» *Diario de Hoy,* El Salvador (10 Aug. 1952).

— *Imagen primera de....* Buenos Aires: Losada, 1945.

— «Imagen Sucesiva de Antonio Machado.» *Sur,* Buenos Aires, 12 (1943).

— «Julio Herrera y Reissig: 18 y 19 de marzo.» *Alfar,* Montevideo, 83 (1943).

— «Ladera de la muerte en la poesía de Julio Supervielle.» *La Nación,* Buenos Aires (January 1933).

— *Libro del mar* (Fotografías de Catalá Roca). Barcelona: Ed. Lumen (1968).

— «Lope de Vega y la poesía contemporánea española.» *Revista Cubana,* Havana, 1 (1935).

— «Mi diario de Punta del Este.» *Tiempo* (18 May 1952).

— «Miedo y vigilia de Gustavo Adolfo Bécquer.» *Bulletin Hispanique,* 70 (1968), pp. 485-509.

— «La miliciana del Tajo.» *El Mono Azul,* 46 (July 1938).

— «Mi última visita al Prado.» *El Mono Azul,* 43 (2 Dec. 1937).

— «En la muerte de Pedro Salinas.» *Tiempo* (13 Jan. 1952).

— «Numancia, tragedia de Miguel de Cervantes.» *El Mono Azul,* 18 (3 May 1937).

— *Poesías completas.* Buenos Aires: Losada, 1961.

— «Picasso y el pueblo español.» *España y la Paz.* México, 43 (1 Sept. 1953).

ALBERTI, Rafael. *La poesía popular en la lírica española contemporánea.* Jean & Leipzig, 1933.
— «El poeta en la España de 1931.» *Patronato Hispano-Argentino de Cultura,* Buenos Aires, No. 8 (1942).
— «Rafael Alberti (artículo autobiográfico).» *La Gaceta Literaria,* 3 (1 January 1929).
— «Un recuerdo para Antonio Machado.» *Biblos,* Buenos Aires, 2 (1943).
— «Sobre Federico García Lorca: *Poeta en Nueva York.*» *Sur,* 10 (1940).
— «Sánchez Mejías, gran matador de toros y autor dramático.» *El Nacional* (9 July 1959).
— *Suma taurina; verso, prosa, teatro.* Barcelona: Editorial RM (1963).
— «Una visita a Santo Domingo de Silos.» *El Nacional* de Colombia (18 Feb. 1960).
ALEIXANDRE, Vicente. «Dos lecturas de Rafael Alberti.» *Insula,* 198, p. 1.
— «Rafael Alberti, pintor.» *El Nacional* (18 July 1957).
ALONSO, Amado. *Materia y forma en poesía.* Madrid: Gredos, 1955.
ALONSO, Dámaso. «Rafael entre su arboleda.» *Insula,* 198 (May 1963), pp. 1, 16.
— *Poetas españoles contemporáneos.* Madrid: Gredos, 1952.
ALQUIÉ, Ferdinand. *The Philosophy of Surrealism.* Ann Arbor, Mich.: Univ. of Michigan Press, 1969.
ASTURIAS, Miguel Angel. «Rafael Alberti, poeta y pintor.» *El Nacional* (19 March 1959).
AUB, Max. «Poesía española contemporánea.» *Cuadernos Americanos,* 1 (Jan.-Feb. 1954), pp. 239-254.
BACHELARD, Gaston. *L'air et les songes.* 3rd ed., Paris: Librairie José Corti, 1959.
— *L'eau et les rêves.* Paris: Librairie José Corti, 1942.
— *La psychanalyse du feu.* Paris: Librairie Gallimard, N.D.
— *Psicoanálisis del fuego.* Trans. Ramón G. Redondo, Madrid: Alianza Editorial, 1966.
— *La terre et les rêveries du repos.* Paris: Librairie José Corti, 1948.
— *La terre et les rêveries de la volonté.* Paris: Librairie José Corti, 1948.
BARY, David. «Sobre el nombrar poético en la poesía española contemporánea.» *Papeles de Son Armadans,* 44 (Feb. 1966), pp. 161-189.
BLANCO-AMOR, Eduardo. «Rafael Alberti, pinta y escribe.» *El Nacional* (19 Aug. 1954).
BLECUA, José Manuel. *El mar en la poesía española.* Madrid: Gredos, 1945.
BODKIN, Maud. *Archetypal Patterns in Poetry.* London: Oxford Univ. Press, 1968.
BÖHL DE FABER, Cecilia. *Cuentos, oraciones, adivinanzas y refranes populares e infantiles.* Leipzig, No. 100, 1878.
BOUSOÑO, Carlos. «La sugerencia en la poesía contemporánea.» *Revista de Occidente,* 20 (Nov. 1964), pp. 188-208.
— *La poesía de Vicente Aleixandre.* 2nd. ed., Madrid: Gredos, 1968.
— *Teoría de la expresión poética.* 5th. ed., I & II, Madrid: Gredos, 1956.
BOUSOÑO, et al. *Seis calas en la expresión literaria española.* Madrid: Gredos, 1951 (pages 253-256 on Alberti).
BOWRA, C. M. *The Creative Experiment.* London: Macmillan, 1949, pp. 220-253.
— *The Heritage of Symbolism.* New York: St. Martin's Press, 1967.
BROWN, Stephen J. *The World of Imagery.* London: Kegan, Parcel, et. al. 1927.
CANO, José Luis. *De Machado a Bousoño.* Madrid: Insula, 1955.
— «La generación poética de 1925.» *Revista Nacional de Cultura,* No. 111 (July-Aug. 1955), pp. 78-79.
— «Machado y la generación poética del 25.» *La Torre,* 12 (Jan.-July 1964), pp. 483-504.
CANO BALLESTA, Juan. *La poesía española entre pureza y revolución (1930-1936).* Madrid: Gredos, 1972.

CARVAJAL, Luis de. «Presencia y ausencia de la nostalgia.» *Tres L*, No. 8, 18 (1941), pp. 105-111.

CARRANZA, Eduardo. «Gracia, misterio y nostalgia de Rafael Alberti.» *Boletín Cultural y Bibliográfico* (Bogotá, Colombia), 10 (1967), pp. 128-148.

CASAS GASPAR, E. *Ritos agrarios, folklore campesino español.* Madrid: 1950.

CASSOU, Jean. *Panorama de la literatura espagnole contemporaine.* Paris: Ed. RRA, 1931.

CASTELLANOS, Ramón. «Alberti: marinero en tierra y poeta en la calle.» *Educación*, 1 (1940), No. 6, pp. 57-60.

CERNUDA, Luis. *Estudios sobre poesía española.* Madrid: Guadarrama, 1957.

CHAMBERLAIN, Vernon A. Galdos' use of yellow in character delineation.» *PMLA*, 79 (1964), pp. 158-163.

CHEVREUL, Michel E. «Exposé d'un moyen de définir et de nommer les couleurs» in *Mémoires de l'Académie des Sciences de l'Institut Impérial de France.* 33 (1861), pp. 3-944.

CIPLIJAUSKAITE, Birute. *El poeta y la poesía.* Madrid: *Insula*, 1966.

CIRLOT, J. E. *A Dictionary of Symbols.* Trans. Jack Sage. New York: 1962.

COHEN, J. M. *Poetry of this Age*: 1908-1965. London: Hutchison Univ. Library, 1966. (Alberti, pp. 185-191.)

CONNELL, G. W. «The Autobiographical Element in *Sobre los ángeles.*» *Bulletin of Spanish Studies*, 40 (1963), pp. 160-173.

— «The End of a Quest: Alberti's *Sermones y Moradas* and the Uncollected Poems.» *Hispanic Review*, 32 (1965), pp. 290-309.

— «A recurring theme in the poetry of Rafael Alberti.» *Renaissance and Modern Studies*, 3 (1959), pp. 95-110.

COSSÍO, J. M. *Los toros en la poesía.* 2nd. ed., Buenos Aires: Losada, 1947.

COVIELLO, A. «Un bienio de poesía en Rafael Alberti.» *Sustancia*, Tucumán, 7-8 (1941), pp. 663-666.

CRESPO, Angel. «Realismo y pitagorismo en el libro de Alberti, *A la pintura.*» *Papeles de Son Armadans*, 30 (1963), pp. 93-126.

CUADROS, Juan José de. «En torno a una alegría: *Verte y no verte* de Rafael Alberti.» *Cuadernos Hispanoamericanos*, 48 (1966), pp. 180-189.

DEBICKI, Andrew. «El 'correlativo objetivo' en la poesía de Rafael Alberti.» *Estudios sobre poesía española contemporánea.* Madrid: Gredos, 1908, pp. 224-261.

DEHENNIN, Elsa. *La resurgence de Góngora et la génération poétique de 1927.* Paris: Didier, 1962.

DIEGO, Gerardo. «La nueva arte poética española.» *Síntesis*, 7 (1929), pp. 183-199.

ELIADE, Mircea. *Images and Symbols.* Trans. Harvill Press, New York: Sheed & Ward, 1961.

ELLIS, Havelock. *The Colour Sense in Literature.* London: Ulyses Book Shop, 1931.

FERNÁNDEZ ALMAGRO, Melchor. «El hombre deshabitado.» *La Voz* (Feb. 1931).

— «Mar de Alberti.» *La Verdad*, No. 58 (8 Sept. 1926).

FERRERES, E. «La generación poética de 1927.» *Papeles de Son Armadans*, 11 (1958), pp. 301-314.

FICHTER, William L. «Color Symbolism in Lope de Vega.» *Romanic Review*, 18 (1927), pp. 220-231.

FLORIT, Eugenio. «La poesía reciente de Rafael Alberti.» *La Torre*, 7 (1959), pp. 11-17.

FOULCHÉ-DELBOSC, R. *Cancionero castellano del siglo XV.* Madrid: 1915.

FRIEDRICH, Hugo. *Estructura de la lírica moderna.* Barcelona: Seix Barral, 1959.

FRYE, Northrup. «Three Meanings of Symbolism.» *Yale French Studies*, No. 9 (1952), pp. 11-19.

SELECTED BIBLIOGRAPHY

La Fuente, Pablo. «Rafael Alberti en Roma.» *Studia Neophilologica*, No. 1436 (1965), pp. 180-182.

Gallego Morell, Antonio. *La generación poética de 1927*. Madrid: Alcalá, 1966.

Gaya Nuño, Juan Antonio. «Carta a Rafael Alberti sobre la pintura.» *Insula*, 198 (May 1963), pp. 3, 14.

Giver Arivau, L. *Folklore de Proaza*. Madrid: Biblioteca de las tradiciones populares españolas, 1886.

González Lanuza, Eduardo. «Crónicas: Homenaje a Rafael Alberti.» *Sur*, No. 281 (1963), pp. 50-62.

— «Rafael Alberti: *Entre el clavel y la espada*.» *Sur*, 10 (1941), pp. 71-76.

González Muela, Joaquín. *El lenguaje poético de la generación Guillén-Lorca*. Madrid: *Insula*, 1955.

— «La poesía de la generación de 1927» in *Pensamiento y letras en la España del siglo XX*. Nashville, Tenn.: Vanderbilt Univ. Press, 1966, pp. 247-256.

— «¿Poesía amorosa en *Sobre los ángeles?*» *Insula*, 80 (1952), p. 5.

Guichot y Sierra, A. *Supersticiones populares recogidas en Andalucía*. Sevilla: Biblioteca de las tradiciones populares españolas, No. 42, 1881.

Guillén, Jorge. *Lenguaje y poesía*. Madrid: Alianza, 1969.

Gullón, Ricardo. «Alegrías y sombras de Rafael Alberti.» *Insula*, 198 (May 1963), pp. 1, 5.

— «Ambiente espiritual de la generación española de 1925». *Revista Nacional de Cultura* 136 (Sept.-Oct. 1959), pp. 28-49.

Horst, Robert Ter. «The Angelic Prehistory of *Sobre los ángeles*.» *Modern Language Notes*, 81 (1966), No. 2, pp. 174-194.

Ibáñez, José Miguel. *La creación poética*. Santiago de Chile: Ed. Universitaria, 1969.

Jacobi, Jolande. *The Psychology of C. G. Jung: An Introduction with Illustrations*. Trans. Ralph Manheim, New Haven: Yale Press, 1943.

Kenyon, Herbert A. «Color Symbolism in Early Spanish Ballads.» *Romanic Review*, 6 (1915), pp. 327-340.

Lewis, C. Day. *The Poetic Image*. London: Cox and Wyman, 1969.

Larralde, Pedro. «El mar, el toro y la muerte.» *Sustancia*, Tucumán, V (1943), pp. 337-353.

Lázaro, Fernando. «La metáfora impresionista.» *Rivista di Letterature Moderne*, 2 (1951), pp. 370-376.

Lozano, Rafael. «Apreciación de Rafael Alberti.» *El Universal, Caracas* (25 Feb. 1960).

Machado, Antonio. «Encuesta a los directores culturales de España. ¿Cómo ven la nueva juventud española?» *La Gaceta Literaria*, 3 (1 March 1929), p. 1.

— «Carta a David Vigodsky.» *Hora de España*, 4 (April 1937).

Mackenzie, D. A. «Color Symbolism.» *Folk-lore*, 33 (1922), pp. 136-169.

Marquina, Rafael. «La batalla de Alberti.» *La Gaceta Literaria* (15 March 1931).

Marrast, Robert. «Rafael Alberti: proses retrouvées (1931-1932).» *Bulletin Hispanique*, 70, No.'s 3-4, pp. 485-509.

Miró, Emilio. «Rafael Alberti: *Poesía (1944-1967)*.» *Insula*, No. 312, pp. 5-7.

Monguió, Luis. «The poetry of Rafael Alberti.» *Hispania*, 43 (1960), pp. 158-168.

Monterde, Alberto. «Inquietudes y medievalismo en la poesía de Rafael Alberti.» *Univ. de Mexico*, 9 (1954), No's 1-2, pp. 8-10, 32.

Morales, Arturo. «Los ángeles en Alberti.» *Carrión*, Puerto Rico, 4 (1935), pp. 325-332.

Morley, S. Griswold. «Color Symbolism in Tirso de Molina.» *Romanic Review*, 8 (1917), pp. 77-81.

Morris, C. B. *A Generation of Spanish Poets*. Cambridge: Cambridge Univ. Press, 1969.

— «Las imágenes claves de *Sobre los ángeles*.» *Insula*, No. 198 (May 1963), pp. 12, 14.

— «Parallel Imagery in Quevedo and Alberti.» *Bulletin of Spanish Studies,* 36 (July 1959), pp. 135-145.

MORRIS, C. B. *«Sobre los ángeles:* a Poet's Apostasy.» *Bulletin of Hispanic Studies,* 37 (1960), pp. 222-231.

NOWOTTNY, Winifred. *The Language Poets Use.* London: The Athlone Press, 1968.

OLIVIO JIMÉNEZ, José. «Medio siglo de poesía española (1917-1967).» *Hispania* 50 (Dec. 1967), pp. 931-946.

ORIBE, Emilio. «Presencia de Rafael Alberti.» *Alfar,* Montevideo, 20 (1942), no page indicated.

PASCO, Allan H. *Proust's Color Vision: A Study of the Use of Color as a Literary Device in 'A la recherche du temps perdu'.* The University of Michigan PhD dissertation, 1968.

PÉREZ, Carlos Alberto. «Rafael Alberti: Sobre los tontos.» *Revista Hispánica Moderna,* 32 (1966), pp. 206-216.

PONCE, Aníbal. «Rafael Alberti y la revista *Octubre.»* *Cursos y Conferencias,* 8, pp. 329-335. N.D.

PREMINGER, Alex. Editor. *Princeton Encyclopedia of Poetry and Poetics.* Princeton: Princeton Press. 1974.

PROLL, Eric. «'Popularismo' and 'Barroquismo' in the Poetry of Rafael Alberti.» *Bulletin of Spanish Studies,* 14 (1942), pp. 59-86.

— «The Surrealist Element in Rafael Alberti.» *Bulletin of Spanish Studies,* 18 (1941), pp. 70-82.

QUIÑONES, Fernando. «Tres toques rápidos a la poesía de Rafael Alberti.» *Cuadernos Hispanoamericanos,* 53 (1963), pp. 524-527.

RÍO, Angel del. *Historia de la literatura.* New York: Dryden Press, 1948.

— *Literatura contemporánea española.* Madrid: Gredos, 1966.

RIVAS SAINZ, Arturo. «Contrapunto y fuga: cuatro compases de Alberti.» *Revista Jaliscience de Literatura,* Guadalajara, July 1943, pp. 29-45.

ROSALES, Luis. «La figuración y la voluntad de morir en la poesía española.» *Cruz y Raya,* No. 38, pp. 65-101.

ROUANET, Leo. *Colección de autos, farsas y coloquios del siglo XVI.* Barcelona: 1901.

SABELLA, Andrés. «La poesía de Rafael Alberti.» *Atenea,* 41 (1940), pp. 273-285.

SALADO, José Luis. «Rafael Alberti, de niño quería ser pintor.» *Cervantes,* Havana (March-April 1931).

SALINAS, Pedro. «Dos elegías a un torero» in *Literatura española del siglo XX.* Madrid: Alianza, 1972, pp. 198-203.

— «La poesía de Rafael Alberti» in *Literatura española del siglo XX.* Madrid: Alianza, 1972, pp. 185-190.

— «Nueve o diez poetas» in *Ensayos de literatura hispánica.* Madrid: Aguilar, 1958, pp. 352-353, 366-368.

SALINAS DE MARICHAL, Solita. *El mundo poético de Rafael Alberti.* Madrid: Gredos, 1968.

— «Los paraísos perdidos de Rafael Alberti.» *Insula,* 198 (May 1963), pp. 4, 10.

SCHULMAN, Ivan A. *Símbolo y color en la obra de José Martí.* Madrid: Gredos, 1960.

SLOTE, Bernice. *Myth and Symbol.* Lincoln, Neb.: Univ. of Nebraska Press, 1963.

SOTO, Fausto. «América y la nueva poesía de Alberti.» *Atenea,* 35 (1936), pp. 448-451.

TEJADA, José Luis. *Rafael Alberti, entre la tradición y la vanguardia.* Madrid: Gredos, 1977.

TORRE, Guillermo de. *Historia de las literaturas de vanguardia.* Madrid: Guadarrama, 1965.

SELECTED BIBLIOGRAPHY

TORRENTE-BALLESTER, Gonzalo. *Literatura española contemporánea (1898-1936)*. Madrid: Aguado, 1949.
— *Panorama de la literatura española contemporánea*. Madrid: Guadarrama, 1956.
TOVAR, Mario. «Alberti nos habla de España.» *Todo*, México, 28 May 1935.
VALBUENA PRAT, Angel. *La poesía española contemporánea*. Madrid: CIAP, 1930.
VALENTE, José Angel: «La necesidad y la musa.» *Insula*, 198 (May 1963), p. 6.
VALLE, Rafael Heliodoro. «Trayectoria de Rafael Alberti.» *Repertorio Americano*, Costa Rica (26 Dec. 1935).
VARELA, Lorenzo. «En el aire sonoro de Rafael Alberti.» *Sol* (28 April 1936).
— «La flauta y el pito; el tambor y el salmo; y la poesía» (en torno a Rafael Alberti). *Taller*, Méjico, 2 (1940), pp. 41-45.
— «Pasión y gracia de Rafael Alberti.» *Romance*, Méjico, 1 (1940), N.P.
VELA, Fernando. «La poesía pura.» *Revista de Occidente*, 41 (1966), pp. 217-240.
VIDELA, Gloria. *El ultraísmo*. Madrid: Gredos, 1963.
VIVANCO, Luis Felipe. «Rafael Alberti en su palabra acelerada y vestida de luces» in *Introducción a la poesía española contemporánea*. Madrid: Guadarrama, 1957.
VOSSLER, Spitzer, et al. *Introducción a la estilística moderna*. Trans. Amado Alonso, Buenos Aires: Imprenta Univ. de Buenos Aires, 1932.
WELLEK, René, and WARREN, Austin. *Teoría literaria*. Trans. Dámaso Alonso, Madrid: Gredos, 1966.
WHEELRIGHT, Phillip. *The Burning Fountain*. Bloomington, Indiana: Indiana Univ. Press, 1954.
WINKELMAN, Ana Marie. «Pintura y poesía en Rafael Alberti.» *PSA*, No. 30 (1963), pp. 147-162.
YAHNI, Roberto. «Sobre: Solita Salinas de Marichal, *El mundo poético de Rafael Alberti*.» *Sur*, No. 320 (1969), pp. 122-123.
ZARDOYA, Concha. «El mar en la poesía de Rafael Alberti» in *Poesía española contemporánea*. Madrid: Guadarrama, 1961, pp. 600-633.
— «La técnica metafórica albertiana» in *Poesía española del 98 y del 27*. Madrid: Gredos, 1968, pp. 294-336.
— «Rafael Alberti y sus primeras poesías.» *Revista Hispánica Moderna*, 30 (1964), pp. 12-19.
ZULETA, Emilia de. *Cinco poetas españoles*. Madrid: Gredos, 1971. (Alberti, pp. 273-396).